To Jo an
appreciation for many rich memories

Henry C. Whyman
June 11, 1993

The Hedstroms and the Bethel Ship Saga

*Methodist Influence on
Swedish Religious Life*

Henry C. Whyman

*With a Foreword by
Kenneth E. Rowe*

Southern Illinois University Press
Carbondale and Edwardsville

Library of Congress Cataloging-in-Publication Data

Whyman, Henry C. (Henry Carl), 1903–
    The Hedstroms and the Bethel Ship saga: Methodist influence
on Swedish religious life / Henry C. Whyman; with a foreword by
Kenneth E. Rowe.
        p.   cm.
    Includes bibliographical references and index.
        1. Hedstrom, Olof Gustaf, 1803–1877.   2. Hedstrom, Jonas.
3. Methodists, Swedish—United States.   4. Swedes—Missions—
United States.   5. Methodist Church—United States—History.
I. Title.
    BX8495.H375W48   1992
    287'.089'397073—dc20   91-39321
    ISBN 0-8093-1762-1   CIP

Frontispiece: Olof Gustaf Hedstrom. Courtesy Drew University
Library, Henry C. Whyman Swedish Methodist Collection.

To
Alice
and in Grateful Memory
Henry Emanuel and Louise Whyman

Contents

Illustrations

Foreword

"The story of the peopling of America has not yet been written. We do not understand ourselves," complained Frederick Jackson Turner in 1891.[1] Subsequent immigration history contributed to national self-understanding. A century later, historians of the Church, as well as of the nation, have turned their attention to a second chapter in the half-told tale of the peopling of America. They have begun to concentrate on the story of the regrouping of citizens along racial, ethnic, and religious lines. The cultural explosion of ethnicity in the 1960s and 1970s called on historians to attend to the long-neglected history of African Americans, Asian Americans, Hispanic Americans, and Native Americans. At the same time, late twentieth-century historians began to reassess their treatment of "older ethnics," the Germans, the Irish, the Italians, and the Swedes, to name only a few. Though these groups have been more or less assimilated in the mainstream of American culture and religion, the full story of their role was often untold in midcentury texts, which stressed white, Protestant, mainline churches as normative. Henry C. Whyman's study of the Hedstroms and the Bethel Ship saga contributes to the rediscovery of the rich diversity of American religious history.

Although the first Swedes settled in Delaware in 1638 shortly after the Pilgrims landed in Massachusetts, they did not come to North America in great numbers until two hundred years later. Between 1840 and 1940 about 1.25 million Swedes emigrated. Although most of the newcomers settled in the Midwest and kept their Lutheran faith, a New York-based Methodist pastor played a crucial role in Swedish immigration. Whyman tells for the first time the remarkable story of Olof Gustaf Hedstrom's mid-nineteenth-century ministry among a steady stream of fellow immigrant Swedes and other Scandinavians.

During the middle years of the nineteenth century, New York harbor teemed with foreign vessels. In the years after 1845, ships of Scandinavian registry were met by a man in a rowboat, Olof Gustaf Hedstrom, who passed out religious tracts and Bibles. Sailors and immigrants alike were invited to visit his floating chapel called "Bethel Ship," or "God's house boat," moored at Pier 11 at the foot of Rector Street on the Hudson River.

Mariner's bethels were organized as special missions in many eastern port cities in the early nineteenth century.[2] Originally designed to provide material and spiritual comforts for seamen during their days in port, their role expanded to welcome wagon and travel agent as immigrants vied with cargo on many ships. All found Hedstrom's welcome warm and his suggestions about the location of rich farmland and fellow Swedes helpful. Others found Hedstrom's rigorous piety attractive, giving Methodists an opening into this largely Lutheran constituency. The converts established Methodist chapels in the farm towns they would settle in the Midwest. In time, their faith found its way back to Europe, establishing Methodism as an alternative to the Lutheran state churches in Denmark, Finland, and Norway as well as Sweden.

Hedstrom's mission to Scandinavian seamen and immigrants in New York harbor was begun in the early 1840s by a Methodist lay preacher, Peter Bergner, a Swedish ship's carpenter converted from a dissolute life through reading Methodist tracts. Bergner could give only part-time to the ministry, so the sponsoring Methodist missionary society looked around for a full-time pastor fluent in Swedish to lead the promising mission. David Terry, the Methodist missionary executive, found a young Swedish convert, Hedstrom, then polishing his English while serving Methodist churches in the Catskills. In May 1845 the Methodist bishop appointed him to the North River Mission.

The mission, later the first Swedish Methodist Church in America, brought many Scandinavian sailors to Christian commitment and Methodist membership. For a time, the ship provided the only Swedish language services of worship in the city. Lutheran hymnals were used, as the Methodists had not yet translated their hymnal into Swedish. In addition, the ship provided an asylum for destitute immigrants, supplying them with bed, table, and wardrobe, as well as a sanctuary. Most important of all, the ship offered English language instruction as well as American geography lessons. A dozen years later (1857) the old ship was replaced by a newer vessel and in 1876 moved to a Brooklyn pier on the East River. Gradually the mission became a church and transferred to the shore.

When Hedstrom died on May 5, 1877, in his seventy-fourth year, the growing work had already reached another stage. Many of the leaders of Scandinavian Methodism in America and in the homeland came from the Bethel Ship mission. The Bethel Ship became the mother church for much of Methodism's ministry to the Scandinavians in the United States, but even more so for Methodism in northern Europe.[3] Through the many sailors who brought their faith back with them to the old country, Methodism gained a foothold in those countries as it did in the "new Swedens" of the Midwest.

Olof Gustaf Hedstrom was born May 11, 1803, in Nottebäck parish of Kronoberg County (Småland) in Sweden. The son of a poor corporal in the Swedish army, he became a tailor's apprentice. At the age of sixteen Hedstrom left home and ended up in the naval city of Karlskrona, where he got a job as secretary for a ship's captain. An international incident brought him to New York City in 1825. Stranded in that city, Hedstrom was forced to return to his old trade. He worked for several years as assistant to a tailor who happened to be an active Methodist; four years later, Hedstrom fell in love with and married his employer's cousin. The young couple experienced evangelical conversion in a Methodist Episcopal church in New York City. In 1833, Olof traveled back to his native land to share his newfound faith with his parents, brothers, and sisters. Shortly after he returned to New York (1835), he offered himself as a candidate for the Methodist ministry.

Swedish Methodism spread with the immigration of Swedish people, especially to the Midwest around Chicago and in Minnesota. A Chicago Swedish mission resulted from revival meetings in 1852. Other churches were organized as far apart as Massachusetts, Texas, and California. Efforts were made to bring the churches together in annual conferences, but this was not accomplished until 1877, when the Methodist Episcopal Church organized the Northwest Swedish Conference, covering work in Illinois and Minnesota. By the time of the First World War, there were four Swedish annual conferences and two mission conferences across the country, with almost twenty thousand members. Along with the Swedish Covenant Church, the Methodists had become a small but significant religious voice alongside the dominant Lutheran Augustana Synod in the Swedish community in America.

As with the Germans, institutions of education, publication, and benevolence were established. Rather than starting new colleges, however, the Swedes concentrated on a theological seminary for training ministers, which was founded in 1870 and moved to Evanston, Illinois, in 1875. In 1934 the Norwegian-Danish Theological Seminary, also in Evanston, was merged with the Swedish Methodist Episcopal Theological Seminary and named the Evanston Collegiate Institute, later to be renamed Kendall College. A weekly church newspaper, the *Sändebudet* (Messenger), began a long series in 1862. Later it became a monthly and continued until 1940, when language conferences were eliminated in Methodist structure. Among Swedish service institutions were Bethany Home and Hospital in Chicago, the Bethel Homes at Ossining, New York, Scandinavian Seamen's Missions in New York and Galveston, Texas, and many camp meetings to serve the revival spirit, which ran strong. Merging of the Swedish language conferences with the English-speaking conferences took place beginning in the 1920s; twenty years later they had disappeared.

To everyone except Swedes, Danes, and Norwegians, Sweden, Denmark, and Norway add up to Scandinavia. The last two, however, even within the Methodist Episcopal church, were acutely conscious of not being Swedes. That feeling was mutual. Hence Methodist work among Norwegians and Danes, although historically related to Swedish development, followed more or less separate organizational patterns. A comprehensive history of Norwegian-Danish Methodism in America was published by Arlow W. Andersen in 1962.[4] While no such study of Swedish-American Methodism has yet been published, Henry Whyman's work on the Hedstroms and the Bethel Ship saga may be considered the first step toward that end.

Henry Carl Whyman was born in Boston in 1903 into a Swedish Methodist parsonage family. Following undergraduate studies at Boston University and New York University, Whyman took the master of divinity degree at Union Theological Seminary in New York. Four years later, in 1937, he completed a doctorate at New York University. His dissertation, not surprisingly, dealt with Swedish-American Methodism.[5] Whyman served several pastorates in the Eastern Swedish Conference and, after merger in 1941, in the present New York Conference. Following a term as district superintendent, Whyman served for many years as executive secretary of the United Methodist City Society, a missionary agency for New York urban ministries. Since retirement in 1973, he has devoted himself to gathering the records of Swedish-American Methodism. We at the United Methodist Archives and History Center at Drew University are much indebted to him.

Kenneth E. Rowe
Professor of Church History
Librarian, Methodist Archives
    and History Center
Drew University

Preface

The story of the Bethel Ship and the Hedstrom brothers is one of the most notable and colorful sagas of Swedish immigrant history. The program of religious and humanitarian services rendered by that floating chapel moored in New York harbor had an incalculable influence upon thousands of arriving immigrants and visiting Scandinavian seamen.

Two earlier histories were written at the turn of the century in the Swedish language, and both describe the expansion of post-Hedstrom Swedish Methodism. Their brief accounts of the Bethel Ship period are valuable but do not do justice to most aspects of early immigrant history. Nor was the biographical information on Olof Gustaf Hedstrom adequately researched and treated.

Some years ago, Dr. Wesley M. Westerberg and I made some preliminary plans to write a book on Swedish Methodism. Both of us had grown up in Swedish Methodist parsonages and had a natural interest in the project. Westerberg's untimely death in 1982 deprived me of a cherished and trusted friend of many years and deprived our project of his scholarly involvement. Subsequently, I decided to confine myself to a study of the Hedstroms—the Bethel Ship saga— their influence during a period of approximately thirty years. It is a story that merits documentation and interpretation. My first treatment of this topic, "Peter Bergner—Pioneer Missionary to Swedish Seamen and Immigrants," was published as an article in the *Swedish Pioneer Historical Quarterly* (30 [1979]: 108–16). It was written in response to comments related to the dearth of available information on Bergner and has been reprinted with permission as chapter 5 in this volume. It is my hope that this book will contribute both to immigrant history and Methodist church history.

This preface provides an opportunity to acknowledge and express appreciation to those to whom I am deeply indebted. Kenneth E. Rowe, professor of church history at Drew University and also Librarian, Methodist Archives and History Center, made research materials available to me. In addition, he read my manuscript and offered useful suggestions. Philip J. Anderson, professor of church history at North Park College and Seminary in Chicago and current president of the Swedish American Historical Society, has been supportive and encouraging in the latter stages of the project leading to publication. Associate director James D. Simmons and managing editor Susan H. Wilson at Southern Illinois University Press have both been extremely helpful. A final reading of the manuscript was done by H. Arnold Barton, professor of history, Southern Illinois University at Carbondale; by Arlow W. Andersen, professor emeritus at the University of Wisconsin-Oshkosh; and by an anonymous reviewer. Their knowledge and editorial comments are appreciated. I am deeply grateful to Carol Wearstler, who prepared the final manuscript with efficiency, accuracy, and always a gracious spirit.

1

The Unintentional Immigrant

On the southern coast of Sweden lies the city of Karls-krona. In the nineteenth century it was a busy little seaport, with access to the Baltic on the east, and on the west, past Denmark, to the Atlantic. In that city in 1825 a young man of twenty-two was employed in a tailor shop. Having been apprenticed ten years earlier, he had learned his trade well and was bright, enterprising, and personable. Before long the almost universal fascination of a seaport, with its sailing vessels arriving from and leaving for worlds beyond the small segment of Sweden with which he had become acquainted, together with the exciting conversations of sailors, fired the young man's imagination. When an unusual opportunity for a sea venture arose, he found it impossible to resist. In doing so, he became a minor player in an episode of international intrigue known in Swedish history as the ill-fated *skeppshandeln* (ship deal).[1]

The young man was Olof Gustaf Hedstrom. The ships for which personnel were being recruited were part of the Swedish navy. The mission involved delivering them to the Republic of Colombia at the port of Cartagena in South America. The circumstances for this somewhat less than honorable arrangement were as follows: Napoleon's marshal, Jean Baptiste Jules Bernadotte, while commander in northern Germany, engaged in negotiation with the Swedes. Sweden's King Gustaf IV abdicated the throne in 1809. Impressed by Bernadotte and desirous of a favorable relationship with Napoleon, Sweden invited Bernadotte to become its crown prince. He became Carl XIV Johan in 1818 but was the virtual ruler as crown prince. The new Swedish ruler favored the

1

acquisition of Norway from Denmark rather than the reconquest of Finland from Russia. He therefore cast his lot with Russia and England against Napoleon and Denmark. The crown prince marched his army into Denmark and forced it to cede Norway in the Treaty of Kiel. Norway, which had declared its independence, was subdued and by a majority vote in the Storting (Parliament) was united with Sweden.

In the course of warfare, Sweden had been forced into a debt it could not repay. The crown prince personally covered the debt and in return the government gave him several naval vessels—ships for which he had no immediate use. On the other hand, Simón Bolívar had liberated areas of South America from Spanish domination and he desired a navy to prevent any attempt by Spain to recapture its former territory. Bolívar's agents had contacted the Stockholm firm of Michaelson & Benedicks. This firm in turn approached Admiral Count Cederström, chief naval officer, with the request that they sell five of the king's ships with full naval equipment to the new Republic of Colombia—all arrangements to be made by the brokerage firm and its name alone to appear on all documents. Carl Johan granted the request. Further, it was to be stated that the ships were desired for a large export transaction with "the East Indies." These arrangements were intended to avoid rupturing a coalition involving Sweden with Russia, Spain, and France.

Olof Hedstrom, after enlistment, was assigned to the 44-cannon frigate *af Chapman*, fully equipped and with a complement of three hundred men. Hedstrom was made secretary to the commanding officer of the ship, Captain C. R. Nordenskiöld, who was later to be elevated to the office of vice admiral. Placed in charge of the whole operation was Baron Carl August Burchard Gyllengranat, destined to become an admiral and secretary of the navy. He was also the captain of *Tapperheten*, first of the vessels to set sail in the summer of 1825. Before the third could get very far, the conspiracy was discovered by Russia and a protest lodged by both Russia and Spain.

On arrival at Cartagena, Captain Nordenskiöld was unable to deliver the ship. The order had been countermanded and he was instructed to sail the *af Chapman* to the port of New York, where it was to be sold. They departed Cartagena in March 1826 and arrived in New York on April 21, 1826. On June 12 they were joined by *Tapperheten*, and later that year the ships were finally sold at auction.[2] The personnel were provided transportation costs for their homeward passage.

Leaving the ship and awaiting one that would return them to Sweden, Hedstrom and some of his companions spent the first night in one of several available sailor's boarding houses. He awakened in the morning to an unpleasant surprise. While asleep, his possessions, including funds for the return passage, had been stolen. Existential circumstances now required that Hedstrom find employment and remain in the United States at least until he had saved sufficient money for the anticipated journey home.[3]

Olof Gustaf Hedstrom was born May 11, 1803, in Tvinnesheda, Nottebäck socken (parish), Kronoberg Län (county) in the province of Småland. He was the son of Corporal Johan Carlsson Hedstrom of the Kronoberg Regiment, an infantry unit, and his wife, Annica Persdotter. The family lived on the Tvinnesheda *soldattorp* (soldier croft). In the territorial army of that time, soldiers were provided by local farmers with cottages and small plots of land. His grandfather, Corporal Carl Hedstrom, had also lived in Tvinnesheda, presumably on the *torp* or croft before him. The family consisted of eight children, six boys and two girls, of whom Olof Gustaf was the third. After the death of his wife in 1822, Corporal Johan Hedstrom married Caterina Nilsdotter, and with her had a ninth child.[4] The corporal is recorded as having retired from military service at the age of forty-nine in 1817, and in 1820 moved to Åseda, a larger community not far to the north. In the Åseda parish record Johan Hedstrom is listed as a *Gratialist*, the term used for one who received an army pension through Vadstena Krigsmanshus (the Armed Services).[5]

We do not know much about the Hedstrom home. The father must have been a responsible parent and with modest resources did the best that he could for his family. Victor Witting says he was described as "an impressive man of The Old School." Those children of whom we have any record seem to have done well in later life. Carl Peter, the oldest, became the owner of a bakery in Lyckeby, and a well-liked, respected member of that community.[6] Olof Gustaf, trained as a tailor, became a renowned Methodist preacher. Jonas J. was trained as a blacksmith, and he too became a Methodist preacher, associated with his brother working with Swedish immigrants in America. Elias S. settled in Detroit, Michigan, where he was a cabinetmaker, and in 1850 his family consisted of a wife and sons Charles and Elias. Further, he owned real estate valued at $2,000.[7] All of the sons seemed to have possessed astute business judgment and abilities.

At the age of twelve, his father arranged to have Olof apprenticed to a tailor. In 1819, at the age of sixteen, the young man left home and moved to Södra Morum, presumably for work after his apprenticeship, and somewhat later found employment in the city of Karlskrona.

The tailor's trade was the one resource upon which the stranded Olof Hedstrom could rely when bereft of his earthly possessions in New York. He found work in an excellent tailoring establishment owned by David Townsend on Division Street. There his skill and industry were quickly recognized. He subsequently became foreman and after marriage went into business for himself on Lewis Street.[8]

Shortly after he began working for Townsend, Olof Hedstrom became acquainted with Caroline Pinckney, Townsend's cousin.[9] Gradually, any further thought of returning to Sweden was abandoned. On January 11, 1829, Olof Hedstrom and Caroline Pinckney were united in marriage.[10]

Caroline Pinckney was born in Mamaroneck, Westchester County, New York, on June 21, 1804.[11] She was of pure Huguenot stock, her ancestors coming from France long before the Revolutionary War (her parents, grandparents, and great-grandparents were buried in the Sleepy Hollow Cemetery at Tarrytown, New York). Peter Pinckney, Caroline's father, had been a Quaker, and her mother embraced Methodism, which became the family religious orientation. The children were nine in number, four boys and five girls. The Pinckney family had moved to New York about 1820 and affiliated with the Second Street Methodist Episcopal Church. Peter Pinckney became a class leader, an important office in early Methodism with responsibility for the spiritual life of fellow members. His class of twenty-seven met weekly in the Pinckney home on the corner of Orchard and Stanton streets, not far from the Second Street Church.[12] The family continued to serve in leadership roles within the church, as evidenced by the frequent appearance of the Pinckney name in Methodist records of that era.

The John Street Church was the mother church of Methodism in New York. As the population of New York City increased and new church buildings were acquired, they were established under the control of the Board of Trustees of the John Street Church as a parent body. In March 1832 Peter Pinckney was elected one of nine trustees—an indication of the esteem in which he was held.[13]

Olof Hedstrom was converted to Methodism about two weeks after his wedding.[14] Caroline's influence is recognized by Swedish Methodist historians and others as the significant factor in this event. She herself had a Methodist conversion experience when she was about twenty-two years of age and had joined the Second Street Methodist Episcopal Church.[15] Olof accompanied his young bride to the Willett Street Methodist Church, and on that occasion had a personal spiritual encounter that determined the future direction of his life. Hedstrom's own account was offered almost four years after his conversion in testimony reported in the *Christian Advocate and Journal* by an anonymous correspondent identified only as "Zero" to its editor, who vouched for the truth of the account:

Messrs Editors:

I attended a love feast last Friday evening in the Willett Street Church, and was not only gratified but exceedingly profited. The many lively and sensible testimonies that were given of Christian and spiritual enjoyments rendered it a feast indeed. . . . But the most interesting of all was the testimony of a Swede, who gave, in substance, the following account: That some years ago, perhaps under the last sermon that the late Dr. Phoebus preached in that house, the truth of God reached his heart, and was the means of his conversion to God. After being himself brought out of darkness into God's marvellous light, he felt such a deep concern for his parents and friends in Sweden, that last May, he took ship and sailed for his native land.[16]

Zero continued to recount Hedstrom's story of his mission to Sweden (see chapter 2). He concluded with a reflection on his "venerable friend, Dr. Phoebus, 'the pioneer of Methodism' . . . for many years a veteran of the cross in this city," whose last sermon should kindle a light in the "dark and cold region of Sweden."

Though Caroline had united with the Second Street Church three years earlier, there was nothing unusual about her attendance at the Willett Street Church. In 1829 there were eight Methodist churches in lower Manhattan, with a total membership of 3,839. All were within reasonable walking distance and were linked together in one circuit. Records were kept on a circuit-wide basis and not for individual churches until a somewhat later period.[17] Members would feel quite at home attending any one of the churches.

Of significance to Zero, as noted, was the fact that Hedstrom's conversion occurred under the influence of Dr. William Phoebus. Long retired after a distinguished career as pastor, publisher of a magazine called *The Methodist*, and conference missionary, his presence might easily have been an occasion of general circuit interest. Indeed, it is quite possible that Caroline took Olof to Willett Street Church because Phoebus was to preach. Dr. Abel Stevens, in his four-volume work, says of him: "He was characterized by a philosophic cast of mind; was an able but not a popular preacher, and possessed literary abilities much superior to the average attainments of his fellow-laborers. . . . His brethren pronounce him, in the Minute obituary, 'a man of great integrity of character, uniformly pious, deeply read in the scriptures, a sound experiential and practical preacher.'"[18]

The ultimate decision was not immediately made. Witting describes Hedstrom's inner struggle as he confronted his life in light of the message that he had heard. Hedstrom eventually found "peace with God after a hard struggle of several hours alone at night in a lumber yard."[19] Caroline often said that from the day of his conversion he never suffered the slightest deviation of spirit.

The service at the Willett Street Church must have seemed strange to Hedstrom, as no musical instruments were permitted in Methodist churches in those days. We have the following description of a service at that church by Samuel A. Seaman:

> The singing was for many years conducted by Joseph Johnson who sat in the body of the church. The state of his mind could always be known by his singing. If he was in a happy frame it would be so fast that it was difficult to keep up with him; but if not, it would be so slow that it was equally difficult to drag along at the same pace. A choir was at length introduced, and on a Sunday morning not long after its appearance the presiding elder (D. Ostrander) occupied the pulpit. He gave out the hymn and the chorister began to play on a bass-viol. "Who brought that fiddle into the church?" shouted the elder; "take it right out!" And he would not preach until it was removed.[20]

The nature of the Methodist church and the religious ambience of the New York religious community generally in the 1820s and 1830s were crucial factors in fashioning Hedstrom's life and ministry. F. Ernest Stoeffler, in his study of

Colonial pietism in early America, finds the Methodist origins in America "a confluence of Puritan and Pietist impulses, the resulting evangelicalism being as closely patterned on its Pietist as on its Puritan model."[21] We shall later deal with Swedish pietism.

The earliest years of Hedstrom's life and relationship to Methodism coincided with that period of history when the Second Great Awakening had its greatest impact upon New York City through the presence and work of Charles Grandison Finney. He came to New York only a few months after Hedstrom's conversion in 1829. Invited by laity prominent in the business and church life of the city, Finney began a revival that lasted almost a year and involved churches of all denominations. He was to return to New York in 1832 and remained there until he became president of Oberlin College in 1835.[22] An appraisal by Sydney E. Ahlstrom of Yale is entirely relevant to New York:

> Finney is an immensely important man in American history by any standard of measure. His revivals were a powerful force in the rising antislavery impulse and in the rise of urban evangelism. He was an influential revisionist in the Reformed theological tradition, an enormously successful practitioner, almost the inventor, of modern high pressure revivalism which, as it spread, would have important consequences for the religious ethos of the nation as a whole.[23]

Hedstrom's ministry both in the Catskills and at the Bethel Ship reflected the Finney influence—in convictions, approach, and spirit. It was first noticeable in his journey to Sweden to convert family and friends in 1833.[24]

One further event in Hedstrom's life needs to be recounted, though the information is limited. The Hedstroms moved to Pottsville, Pennsylvania, where Olof opened a tailor establishment. New York Methodist Episcopal membership rolls record that in November 1830, Oloff [*sic*] and Caroline Hedstrom were removed by certificate of transfer. One account states that he "opened a clothing store in Pottsville, Pa., where he had great success." Witting, on the other hand, reports that it was clearly not the will of God that Hedstrom should become a businessman since the Pottsville business hardly supported itself.[25] He further indicates that in 1833, Hedstrom sold the store and traveled to Sweden. All the evidence we have establishes that Olof Hedstrom had retained his New York establishment and was financially comfortable. Whatever the fiscal success of the project may or may not have been, there seems to be no doubt that Hedstrom was in a state of ambivalence. He was struggling with an urgent sense of responsibility for the spiritual welfare of family and friends in Sweden.

Though little is written about Hedstrom's family life, an occasional glimpse reveals it to have been serene and devout. Witting states that their forty-eight-year marriage was "exceedingly happy."[26] Sven B. Newman arrived in New York in late January 1851 to become Hedstrom's first ministerial associate on the Bethel Ship. Invited to stay with the Hedstrom family at 4 Carlisle Street, he became acquainted with their children, Maria Elisabeth, an adopted daughter, and Wilbur Fisk, a son.[27] We know of no further reference to Maria Elisabeth. The son was given the name of an influential Methodist preacher and educational leader. Dr. Wilbur Fisk became president of Wesleyan University in 1830, after twice declining election to the office of bishop in order to continue development of educational institutions within Methodism. He was the first Methodist minister in the East to have the benefit of collegiate training, having graduated from Brown University with honors.[28] Methodist annals record an impressive series of sermons by Fisk in New York at a so-called Four Day Meeting in January 1831.[29] Wilbur Fisk Hedstrom was later enrolled in Ashland Collegiate Institute, a Methodist institution within the Windham (New York) Circuit served by Olof Hedstrom.[30] Two years later we learn through the *Christian Advocate and Journal* that "Wilbur Fisk Hedstrom, of Greenville, son of Rev. O. G. Hedstrom, Swedish Missionary," was married to Harriet, daughter of A. C. Judson, Esq., of Prattsville.[31] He became a physician and practiced in New Jersey.

There were also periods of sadness in the Hedstrom home. We are reminded of the high incidence of infant mortality prevalent in the middle of the nineteenth century. After the birth of Wilbur, nine children were born, all of whom died in early years. Though there is no known reference to these tragic events by either Olof or Caroline Hedstrom, a public announcement was carried by the *Christian Advocate and Journal* in 1841: "April 1st, at Greenwell (Greenville) Green County, N.Y., of scarlet fever, Mary E., daughter of Rev. O. G. Hedstrom and Caroline Hedstrom, age 3 years and 11 months."[32]

2

Steps Toward the Methodist Ministry

On May 27, 1833, Olof Gustaf Hedstrom boarded the brig *Standard*, bound for Bremen. The ultimate destination was Sweden, his first return to his native land from which he had departed eight years earlier. He took with him a well-bound book of blank pages upon which he intended to write a travel journal.[1] Unfortunately, the journal is less complete than we should desire. The entries are sporadic and end with his arrival at his brother's home in Lyckeby, Sweden. For information about succeeding events, we are dependent upon reports made following his return to New York.

The journal is nonetheless a valuable resource for a study of Olof Gustaf Hedstrom. There could not be many (if any) such diaries of a returning Swedish immigrant as early as 1833. In addition to its rarity, it is the only diary Hedstrom ever kept, so far as is known. Like all autobiographical statements, it is self-revealing. We see the intensity of his spiritual commitment and the rigid standards by which he lived. From the very beginning Hedstrom considered the journey a missionary venture in every respect. There are also intimations that he received confirmation of the direction in which his life would move. His Sweden experiences, with satisfying and successful results, erased all doubts and confirmed his timid impulse toward Christian mission. No longer would he be satisfied with a business career in the clothing industry.

The desire to visit his family in Sweden is understandable. He had left suddenly and probably without taking appropriate farewell—doubtless with the intention of a reasonably early return. As communication between the continents was difficult, there had been no contact between Hedstrom and his family during his eight years in America. We have earlier described Hedstrom's conversion, which was impressed with the accompanying responsibility to seek the conversion of others. Inevitably his thoughts went to his father and other family members.

Parting from his wife and friends was a painful experience. Transatlantic travel in those days was filled with hazards and uncertainty. His first entry in the diary is poignant:

New York, Monday, May 27, 1833

This day has been a solemn day to me. This morning I was very much affected in my family worship. Previous to prayer, I was thinking of the solemn moment before me. I was thinking of a kind companion that I was about to leave, the many Christian friends that visited me, and the blessed means of grace that I should be deprived of and the probability of never again enjoying any of these blessings. I was in some measure overcome in my feelings. I endeavored to suppress my feelings as far as I could before my wife. I was very much blessed while in prayer.

About 9 o'clock in the forenoon, we got a man to take my things on board. Mr. Johns, a young man of excellent principle and, I believe, a Christian who occupied my store, asked me if we should have a word of prayer before I left. We called our friends together and sang a verse or two and I prayed. I felt the Lord very precious and was melted in tears and tenderness. Then Mr. Johns prayed and we felt truly that the Lord was with us. Now my departure was at hand. I went out of the house as soon as possible for fear that my feelings should overcome me. May the Lord bless and be with her and reward her for all her kindness and affection that she exhibited toward me since our union together. And if the Lord shall take me before I return to my family, may we meet where partings and sorrows shall never come.[2]

Leaving his home with the man who had agreed to convey his baggage to the dock where the *Standard* was moored, he "preached Jesus to him all the way" and observed that he seemed much moved.

Once the passengers boarded, the vessel was hauled out into the stream in preparation for an early departure the next morning. However, the next two days were stormy, and contrary winds delayed their departure until Thursday morning, May 30. Hedstrom's traveling companions, including the captain and the mate, treated him with respect, but there was "no mark of Jesus about them." Their language was sometimes offensive. They politely offered him a drink and always drank to his health. Hedstrom immediately established his Christian identity. "I, in a solemn manner have told them that I do not drink any liquor, for conscience sake." In his mind they became subjects for his mission: "I see here is something for me to do. The Lord give me grace and may I be wise as a serpent and harmless as a dove."

On Tuesday, in good humor in spite of the delay, the captain and Hedstrom became engaged in a friendly conversation about the weather and other topics of a general nature. In the course of the conversation Hedstrom shared his thoughts on the disastrous personal and social consequences of alcohol. The captain, conceding the truth of that which had been said, indicated that Hedstrom was indeed fortunate to be in full control of his appetites. His remark, "I wish I could," was an open door for a discussion of the power of religious faith and prayer.

A day later at dinner, taking a small glass, the captain smiled at Hedstrom and said he thought he could find biblical support for it. When challenged, he reached for his Bible and thumbed its pages without much success. He was no match for Hedstrom, who quoted chapter and verse. The captain good-naturedly conceded Hedstrom's superior biblical knowledge.

Finally, on May 30, early in the morning, the *Standard* set sail. Several persons were, in later years, to comment upon Hedstrom's power of graphic description in his sermons. His mind was acutely visual. The picture of New York and its harbor, as seen from the ship's decks as they departed, was so vividly impressed upon his mind that three weeks later he could reproduce it in his journal:

It was a beautiful morning; the scenery was very pretty; interesting sights was [*sic*] to be seen on every hand. Looking down toward Sandy Hook I saw the beautiful banks on the side of the river, which was [*sic*] adorned with forts, mansion houses, gardens and green fields, etc.; and looking over the water the large number of vessels of almost every size, some sailing up and some sailing down the river; then I saw the various flags blowing in the breeze and the feeling all these objects produced in me was that they harmonized with the beautiful scenery. While standing almost lost in thoughts concerning the great variety of objects and their various relations I turned around and fixed my eyes toward the city and beholding the towering steeples and splendid houses; the Castle Garden with its green trees; and looking up along the docks the vast number of ships and vessels and flags of almost every nation, and so far as my eye could see up the North River it appeared like an extensive forest; and now and then Steam boats passing majestically up and down the rivers in every direction round this greatest metropolis in America.[3]

There is no journal entry between May 29 and June 21. On the latter date his opening sentence is adequate: "The Lord has seen good to lay his afflicting hand upon me in consequence of which I have not able [*sic*] to keep my journal since the 29th of May." He does say that he had spent blessed seasons in solitude contemplating God's providential care during the eight years since leaving Sweden.

On Sunday, June 23, traveling up the English Channel, Hedstrom had his first clear view of land. Again, we note the visual quality of his mind. He made three sketches—a part of the Seven Cliffs, Beth Head with lighthouse and telegraph station, and the narrows of the English Channel with the English and French coasts.

The North Sea, with its capricious weather and wind, caused navigational problems and tense moments. Caught in a dead calm, with a strong current driving the vessel toward shore, Hedstrom prayed: "Regard us in mercy and give us wind and I should consider [it] as a new token that I was called of the Lord to go to Europe." His early sense of assurance of answered prayer was followed by an uncomfortable feeling that he was trifling with God and exaggerating his own importance. However, a breeze soon made it possible to sail out to sea. Obviously, Hedstrom was still grappling for confirmation that his mission was God's call.

Traveling through Germany—Bremen, Hamburg and Lübeck—was an enriching educational experience.[4] Hedstrom was particularly interested in the medieval architecture, the steep rooflines, the gabled setbacks, the sculptured ornamentation. He was struck by the beauty of the tree-lined streets. The cathedral in Bremen impressed him. Its history was told to him by the American consul, upon whom he called to obtain a passport, including the information that the church was built in 1091, and the first service conducted by Archbishop Adelbent (Adelbert). The consul had been appointed forty years earlier and proudly displayed his commission by Gurl (George) Washington.

Hedstrom arrived in Hamburg on Sunday morning, June 30, at 9:30. He was disappointed to discover that there was no afternoon or evening religious service that he might attend. The only service was at eleven o'clock, and he apparently felt he needed to refresh himself after the night's travel. He was invited to attend a theater performance in the evening, of significance because the king of Denmark and Holstein would be a special guest. This invitation to an event that desecrated the Sabbath was instantly rejected. Hedstrom would undoubtedly have considered a theater performance sinful in any circumstance. However, between eight and nine o'clock that evening a parade of lancers and regimental officers escorting the royal persons with considerable pomp and ceremony passed the hotel. Hedstrom's description of the king of Denmark, Frederik VI, was unflattering: "an old, etc., of small stature."

On Monday night, Hedstrom shared a carriage on the way to Lübeck with a Swedish gentleman and his lady, a Dutch baroness. Traveling through the night, they conversed. His countryman could speak in several languages and on almost any subject with one exception, vital religion, the subject Hedstrom was most interested in pursuing. The conversation gradually drifted into silence as the night wore on.

Embarking a steamship at Lübeck, Hedstrom sailed for Copenhagen. Before arriving, he caught his first glimpse of his homeland. Tedious custom and passport formalities caused annoying delays. When finally they set forth, contrary winds slowed their passage and they did not arrive at Landskrona, Sweden, until 1:00 in the morning. No personnel were available to process his entry. He was taken to a small tavern that served the Swedish garrison protecting the harbor. Hedstrom was respectfully received and introduced to the commanding officer. He was provided a couch in a small room, but felt extremely uncomfortable, as he had seen some evidence that the tavern was used as a house of ill repute. Probably remembering his first night at the seamen's inn in New York, Hedstrom dared not go to sleep, fearing that he might be robbed. Daylight in the northern land came early at this time of year. He arose and walked along the banks of the harbor until the appropriate officials were available to process his entrance.

The morning was beautiful. Walking along the green banks of his native soil was, for Hedstrom, an exhilarating experience.

> As I look around and saw the trees, etc., peculiar to my native soil my heart was uplifted to heaven in gratefulness for the inumerable [sic] mercies of God bestowed on me in the years since I left this my native land. I love it, and it seems to animate my feelings to walk once more on its green banks. While walking I held, as it were, conversation with myself what God had done for me, and especially what he had done for my soul . . . and as I have not had the rational doubt on my mind but that it was my duty to go and see my relations and with the help of the Lord do what I could for God and their immortal souls, I felt to proceed on my journey as soon as I could.[5]

At eight o'clock on the morning of July 5, Hedstrom had been cleared by the authorities and was ready to continue his travel through Sweden. There were no established stagecoach routes at that time; the only means of travel was by hired horse and carriage. The distance between one point or station and the next was about five miles. Since Hedstrom was in Sweden, we must assume that this reference is to "Swedish" miles—one such mile being the equivalent of six English miles—or about thirty miles.

Soon he arrived at the university city of Lund and registered at a hotel while awaiting a fresh horse and carriage to advance him on his journey. A small company of men in conversation immediately recognized Hedstrom as a foreigner and inquired where he was from. At least two were Lutheran pastors. Learning that he came from America, they were eager to question him. Their political questions were dealt with by Hedstrom in his journal hurriedly in one sentence: "They asked me if Genl. Jackson was President yet, etc." In answering their questions with regard to religion, he was far more expansive. He explained to them that though civil laws in America were predicated on Christian principles, there was complete separation of church and state, in contrast to the Swedish system of an established church. Church membership was a voluntary choice, but was subject to moral and spiritual standards, rigidly adhered to. "I told them that so long [*sic*] people swore and lived a wicked life they cannot belong as members of our Christian societies." Since in their jocular conversation there had been a fair amount of profanity, this comment was undoubtedly intentional. Hedstrom states that he heard no profanity from the ministers, but neither was there reproof. They shared in the common laughter. In the matter of ministerial salaries, it was pointed out that in America no support came from the government, but was determined and paid by local congregations.

It is apparent that Hedstrom was aware of some discomfort on the part of the group. He states: "One of them politely took his leave and as I told them our Christians endeavored to live a holy life they seemed to be very silent." However, as the group dispersed, one member desired to speak with Hedstrom further. He identified himself as a Lutheran pastor serving as an agent for the Temperance Society of Sweden. He had come from Stockholm to meet with the bishop of the Lund Diocese about an appointment to a parish church. The Temperance Society had increased its membership considerably. He was interested in knowing how the movement fared in America. Hedstrom, reflecting his experience, informed him that "almost all Christians in America belong."

From him, Hedstrom was eager to inquire about the strength of the *läsare* movement. This is the first instance in which we learn Hedstrom was familiar with the pietistic movement in Sweden which, in derision, had come to be known as *läsare* (reader). In defiance of the state-established Conventicle Edict, small groups of persons gathered in private homes for Bible reading, prayer, and mutual spiritual support that they often failed to find in a sterile church establishment. In reply to Hedstrom's inquiry, the pastor stated that he estimated their numbers to be about six thousand committed *läsare*, or pietists. Asked what he thought of them, the pastor's response was first ambivalent and slightly inclined toward ridicule. When Hedstrom proclaimed that he identified with them, the tone of his conversation changed. Though he was a Lutheran pastor, he often attended their meetings and felt they were good people. As they were about to depart, the pastor politely asked "if I would not take a little wine and water with him which I did and bade him adieu."

From Lund, Hedstrom traveled across southern Sweden to the town of Lyckeby, in the neighborhood of Karlskrona, from which he had sailed for South America. His compelling urgency is reflected in the comment: "I travelled nearly night and day and with uplifted heart to the Lord to direct my journey so that I might find my oldest brother Carl Peter who lived fifty miles from where my father lived when I left Sweden."[6] The journey was accomplished in less than two days.

Carl Peter was important to his missionary design. We learn for the first time, as we read the journal, that a member of the Hedstrom family had been influenced by the *läsare* movement. "As he had found the Lord before I left I hope he had proven faithful and it would be a double joy to see each other. As a Christian he would give me all the information necessary for to lay plans for my further journey in what way would do the most good."[7]

Sunday morning, June 7, Hedstrom began his journey at two o'clock with the intention of arriving in Lyckeby early in the forenoon. However, he had been obliged to wait for his conveyance and was therefore delayed. Additionally, he was determined to fulfill an obligation en route. When they arrived at Nättraby, four miles from Lyckeby, Hedstrom, with some difficulty, prevailed upon the driver to make what must have been a relatively short detour. Back in New York, Hedstrom had had a young man, J. P. Granat, in his employ with whom he had been in association for four years. This young man "had found the Lord in happy America." Hedstrom carried a letter from Granat to his parents, who lived in the area. He knew the joy with which it would be received and also the joy that the son would experience with tidings from his parents on Hedstrom's return to America "if the good Lord spare my life."

Approximately halfway there was a fork in the road and they were uncertain which way to take. They saw a man and woman walking and inquired concerning directions to the Granat residence. The couple came closer to the carriage and announced that their name was Granat. Hedstrom asked if they had relatives in America and it was readily established that they were J. P. Granat's parents. The letter was delivered and Hedstrom told them that he had seen their son six weeks earlier. As can well be imagined, the encounter was deeply emotional: "I can never forget with what heartfelt emotion these parents expressed themselves. As I take leave of them their eyes were full of tears of thankfulness for my kindness."

Approaching Lyckeby within the hour, Hedstrom was not at all sure he would be able to find his brother. He could have moved—even died. At the very least he hoped to secure some information about him. Seeing two lads, he asked if they knew Charles (the journal uses the anglicized form of Carl) Hedstrom. There was a moment of hesitation as the boys looked at him with some astonishment, until one exclaimed: "Lord God, here is his brother." He was told where the brother lived and that he was the owner of a bakery—something of a surprise to Hedstrom, since his brother had known nothing about baking when Olof had left Sweden.

It was eleven o'clock when they arrived at the brother's home. Carl Hedstrom and his wife were at church, but would be expected momentarily. The servant girl who had opened the door was reluctant to admit him without authorization. However, when Hedstrom identified himself as Carl's brother, he was permitted to enter. An old lady opened a door to an adjoining room and invited him in. She introduced herself as Carl's mother-in-law and pointed to a little girl about eight months old, who she said was Carl's daughter. Olof's attempt to surprise his brother and to see if he was still recognized was thwarted. Word of his arrival had reached Carl and his wife before they reached home. The brothers tearfully embraced and "gave praise to the Lord together for His preserving care."

The preeminent question on Olof's mind was asked: "I felt most anxious to know if he had the blessed evidence as he had eight years ago that the Lord was precious to his soul." The answer was affirmative, and further, "his wife and mother-in-law who lived with them also knew the reality of religion."

The brothers spent the rest of the day sharing their experiences over the years and catching up on family news. Olof was to learn that several of the family had died in the intervening years—Johannes, one of the youngest of his brothers; a dear sister, Johanna; his grandmother; and his stepmother. The day was ended with devotions, each brother offering prayers. Olof writes: "I was melted to tenderness before the Lord as my dear brother addressed the throne of grace in his way though he made use of prayers that he had learned out of the

Lutheran prayer book, but he prayed from sincerity of his heart and I was very blessed."[8]

The journal closes with an entry—mainly contemplative—on Monday, July 8. Hedstrom writes of the refreshing sleep in a good bed after the arduous journey over Sweden in a roughly built cart. He wanders in and out of his brother's very comfortable house and walks through his beautiful orchard, all of which revealed "the blessing of heaven and an industrious husbandman." He noted his brother's business success and the preference bestowed on him due to his reputation for honesty in his dealings. He is distressed that in a beautiful land those who through repentance and faith have found the Savior should suffer scorn and persecution, particularly from some preachers.

Hedstrom arrived back in New York aboard the *Minerva* on October 17, 1833.[9] The Swedish port of embarkation was Gävle. Assuming approximately five weeks for the return journey, we can surmise that he left Sweden in early September. Were it not for an extemporaneous account offered by Hedstrom at an informal weeknight service in late December of that year, which was reported in the *Christian Advocate and Journal* under the rubric "The Love Feast and the Swede,"[10] we would have been left without specific knowledge of the missionary's activities during the approximately two-month sojourn following the last entry in his journal. The fact that the pages are blank after his departure from his brother's home suggests Hedstrom's major preoccupation with the central purpose of the journey.

The visit to his father, then a retired army corporal threescore years old, was an emotional reunion. Olof "embraced him in his arms with so much affection, and such earnest solicitude for his soul, that he . . . yielded to his entreaties, and was persuaded to seek salvation through faith in the blood of the Lamb."[11]

Hedstrom visited and conversed with other relatives with satisfying results. He expanded his missionary work to include a number of other towns and villages in the general area of his native home, speaking to all with whom he found an opportunity for personal evangelistic work and always stressing the nature and importance of an experiential religion. Considerable numbers of persons listened with serious interest. The response was generally positive.

The night before Hedstrom's departure provided an unforgettable climactic experience. Several persons had requested an opportunity to come together for a farewell visit with him. Arrangements were made to receive them in his uncle's home. Word had apparently been passed around and fifty or sixty persons crowded the home. Among those present was the most influential man in the community. After they had been seated or accommodated in some fashion, Hedstrom spoke to them as a group. He began by describing the place of the church and religion in American life. This account would certainly have included the nature of personal religion as practiced in American Methodism of that era, as well as in other denominations. He related his own immigrant experiences and the circumstances leading to his religious experience and church relationship.

He closed his remarks of a more general nature with the proposal that he take his leave of them by speaking individually to each person present regarding his or her views on religion. He confronted each one with a question concerning a personal relationship with God and expectations of obtaining eternal life. The experience became so moving that before he was halfway through, many were in tears. The meeting lasted until twelve o'clock.

The next morning a number came to see him before he departed. Some were weeping and confessing their sins. They were anxious to know what they must do to be saved. The wife of the town's leading citizen was eager to share with Hedstrom the knowledge that her husband had inaugurated family worship that morning. Messages were received by Hedstrom after his arrival home with information that the sown seed was flowering in conversions and an awakening spirit.

Hedstrom was accompanied on his homeward journey by two younger brothers—Jonas, aged nineteen, and Elias, aged seventeen. Nils William Olsson, an authority on Swedish immigration, records no passengers on the *Minerva* other than the three brothers when it docked in New York.[12] The correspondent writing in the *Christian Advocate and Journal* reported that one had been converted during the sea voyage and was now a member of a Methodist class in the city. The other had been converted shortly after his arrival in New York.[13]

Elias is listed in the official Methodist Church records as a member of a class related to the Second Street Church, which met on Tuesday evenings under the leadership of John C. Helme.[14] There is no mention of the name Jonas Hedstrom in New York Methodist records. It seems that his stay in New York was relatively short. We next hear of him in Illinois, having arrived from Pennsylvania.

Hedstrom returned from Sweden exhilarated by his experiences. He began immediately to take a more active role in the leadership of the church. The account of "The Love Feast and the Swede," published in the widely circulated Methodist weekly, must have enhanced his reputation as an effective spiritual advocate. There is no known explicit statement by Hedstrom of his intention or desire to become a Methodist minister. However, encouraged by those responsible for his election and appointment to positions of leadership, Hedstrom accepted every new opportunity that inevitably led in that direction.

The first official post Hedstrom held was that of "exhorter." This post was bestowed by recommendation of the class to which he belonged, or by the stewards who administered the spiritual program of the church. The preacher was expected to examine the candidate before awarding the certificate, an exhorter's license. This must have occurred shortly after his return to the States. Approximately six months after that arrival, on April 22, 1834, Olof G. Hedstrom was granted a local preacher's license by vote of the New York District of the Methodist Episcopal Church, on recommendation of the East

Circuit of that district. This license was only the first step toward ordination and membership in a regional conference, through whose bishop he would be assigned to a circuit. The granting of the license did not automatically lead to a ministerial career. The function was primarily local in nature. The book *Discipline* of the Methodist Episcopal Church at that time stated that the district conference awarded local preacher's licenses to candidates recommended by local churches, "when in the judgment of said Conference, their grace and usefulness warranted."[15]

On July 23, 1834, Hedstrom was appointed a class leader. The Hedstroms had from the beginning of their active church membership in 1829 been assigned to a class whose leader was John Deveau. That class was divided, and Olof Hedstrom was given responsibility for leadership of a group of persons. In the record of the East Circuit class membership, there is a notation beside names indicating those who were transferred to O. G. Hedstrom's class. This class met on Friday evenings in the Sunday school room of the Second Street Methodist Episcopal Church.[16]

The class was an integral part of the program of Wesleyan Methodism from its beginnings in the eighteenth century. Its purpose was the spiritual enhancement of every church member. In the preface of his recently published scholarly study, David L. Watson defines its role as conceived by John Wesley: "What mattered to them (John Wesley and his preachers) was that people who had met the challenge of Christian discipleship in their lives, whatever the stage of their spiritual pilgrimage, should have a means of mutual support. The class meeting was the essential referent for early Methodist committment."[17] A *Discipline* operative when Hedstrom was appointed defines one of the duties of a class leader. "Let each Leader carefully enquire how every soul of his Class prospers: not only how each person observes the outward rules, but how he grows in the knowledge and love of God." This required preparation on the part of the leader. Class leaders were therefore directed to "such a course of reading and study as shall best qualify them for their work, especially let such books be recommended as will tend to increase their knowledge of the scriptures, and make them familiar with those passages best adapted to Christian influence. Whenever practicable, let the preachers examine the Leaders in the studies recommended."

The following year Olof G. Hedstrom was received "on trial" into the New York Conference of the Methodist Episcopal Church. The conference convened at the Sand Street Church, Brooklyn, on May 6, 1835, under the presidency of Bishop John Emory. In the record of Hedstrom's East Circuit class, beside his name there is a notation dated May 23, 1835, "Removed as Circuit Preacher." At the final session of the conference, Hedstrom received his first pastoral appointment, which was to the Charlotte Circuit in upstate New York, about which we shall write more in the next chapter.[18]

Hedstrom's timid and hesitant inclination toward a ministerial career two or three years earlier had now matured into a firm conviction. The last two years with which this chapter has dealt had been a time of testing. Hedstrom's missionary journey to his native land had strengthened his decision to move forward. Returning to the States after the exhilarating experience, Hedstrom had actively assumed leadership roles in his local church. Each new responsibility brought guidance and counsel from his own pastor and ministerial leaders in the district and conference.

Earlier self-doubts disappeared—his ministerial career was about to be launched following his appointment as a probationary member of the conference. However, there were further steps and procedures leading to full ordination and conference membership. As a probationary member, Hedstrom would be evaluated for two years. Though the Methodist church had moved to establish educational institutions beginning in 1820 and the need for intellectual standards was gradually becoming a consideration, it was still common practice to make "gifts, graces and usefulness" the primary qualifications.

Further, the Methodist book *Discipline* mandated a course of study for ministerial candidates covering a four-year reading and study program under the supervision of a board of examiners. The first year of study had been passed by Hedstrom, along with a recommendation by the district conference, before he could be approved for membership "on trial." The record shows that Olof G. Hedstrom was received into the New York Conference in full connection and ordained a deacon by Bishop Beverly Waugh at the Washington Street Church in Brooklyn on May 17, 1837.[19] The following year Bishop Hedding ordained Hedstrom an elder at the 1838 session of the New York Conference held at the Greene Street Church in New York.[20]

We now turn to Hedstrom's first appointment as a ministerial member of the New York Conference.

3

The Circuit Rider

Olof G. Hedstrom became a circuit rider: his first appointment after his acceptance as a probationary ministerial member of the New York Conference of the Methodist Episcopal Church was to the Charlotte Circuit in the northern foothills of the Catskill Mountains. From the beginning the Methodist ministry was an "itinerant" ministry, with ministers moving from place to place with frequency. During the course of the ensuing ten years, Hedstrom rode six different circuits of the Catskill region as recorded in the official journal of the New York Conference:

    1835–36—Charlotte
    1836–38—Jefferson
    1839–40—Coeymans
    1841   —Windham
    1842   —Catskill and Burham
    1843–44—Prattsville[1]

The picture of a pioneer preacher on horseback, dressed in the coarse cloth of a wilderness traveler, his saddlebags filled with Bibles and Christian literature, symbolizes an early era in American history. The system of circuit riders was devised to make certain that the Gospel followed the migrating pioneers in their westward trek to tame the wilderness and settle in virgin territory. The Methodist itinerant preacher traveled from settlement to settlement, preaching to those who would listen, seeking to meet their spiritual needs, and gathering those so disposed into little Methodist classes, hopefully in time to become Methodist societies.

With the passage of time, the circuits became structured to compose a number of preaching points, or places, within a clearly defined geographical area. The preaching place of a circuit differed in their stages of development. Some in older stable communities were established churches; others had the potential of becoming a church; and still others, in less populated rural areas, were only informal classes. In all cases the purpose was to preach the Gospel and win converts. The meeting places were modest and simple, church buildings or school houses, private homes, barns, and a variety of rented or borrowed facilities.

The circuits varied in geographic size depending upon population and how villages were clustered. In the Catskill Mountains region, the Jefferson Circuit, when it was formed out of the Sharon Circuit in 1821, had a circumference of about four hundred miles to be served by two circuit riders. However, the circuits were in continual process of rearrangement as need and personnel required, with manageability its goal. The Jefferson Circuit was the second circuit to be served by Hedstrom, though as we shall see, he came to know it very early in his Catskill Mountain ministry. The number of preaching places also varied. When established, the Jefferson Circuit had forty-two preaching places, according to a reliable source.[2] The Windham Circuit, later to be served by Hedstrom, had about eighteen preaching places at that time, as recalled by Daniel Steele who, as a young man, frequently traveled with Hedstrom.

The Charlotte Circuit was much more compact. It was only one year old when Hedstrom was appointed, having been formed out of the Delaware Circuit in 1834. Sometimes called the Charlotte Valley Circuit, it covered the territory along the Charlotte River, a tributary running southeast into the Susquehanna River at Oneonta. At that time, preaching places were Charlotteville, Russ Hill, Dugway, South Worcester, Fergusonville, East Davenport, Davenport Centre, Briar Street, West Davenport, and the Hemlocks.[3]

When the new preacher arrived on the Charlotte Circuit in late May of 1835, his first obligation was to find housing for himself and his family. There was no parsonage on the circuit at this early period of its development. The prevailing custom of a circuit committee appointed for the purpose of making adequate housing arrangements for the preacher seems not to have been implemented at Charlotte. Edward White, who traveled the Catskill Mountain circuits at a much later time, was interested in preserving some of its colorful history. In writing of the Charlotte Circuit, he provides the following account:

> Mr. Hedstrom lived at the place now known as Fergusonville, in a building formerly used as a wash-house and wood shed. When he moved there the place was without a single article of furniture, save an old cracked stove. The preacher had no money with which to buy such things as he needed, but he was equal to the emergency, and taking some rough boards and a few round sticks from his woodpile he made a table, a bedstead, a cupboard, and a few benches for seats, and when the work was done he knelt down and thanked God that he could count himself happy in the possession of such a comfortable shelter from the storm.[4]

Hedstrom's experience was not unique. About twenty years earlier another circuit preacher, Heman Bangs, told of the housing problem when he came to the Sharon Circuit. After a long search, all he could find was a long-abandoned dwelling that had been used first as a sheepcote and then as a cooper's shop. He took mud from the road to fill the cracks and whitewashed the interior. "Here I put my young wife and one child, frequently leaving them for two weeks at a time: but there was no complaining; we had given all for Christ, and were content."[5] Hedstrom shared the heroic tradition of ministry on the frontier.

In the beginning, the Hedstroms must have felt lonely in their new situation and makeshift residence. Both were acclimated to the city of New York, though Olof had known the life of smaller villages of Sweden, and Caroline, in childhood, had lived in the neighboring village of New Rochelle. Both had resided briefly in Pottsville, a Pennsylvania village, but had returned to New York. A friend and colleague was later to write: "The year 1835 was the first of [Hedstrom's] itinerant labors, and the transition was great from his lucrative business and religious privileges in the city of New York, to the forest-clad hills of Delaware county."[6]

He was not to remain a lonely stranger for long. The friend referred to above was the first colleague to pay the Hedstroms a visit in their humble rustic cottage shortly after they were settled. He was Elbert Osborn, who had been appointed to the adjacent Jefferson Circuit with two associates, John Bangs and R. H. Bloomer, also in 1835. Osborn was well acquainted with the area, having served neighboring circuits that had included preaching points in the Charlotte Circuit.

Osborn had heard the story of the remarkable conversion of Olof G. Hedstrom and was delighted at his appointment to the Charlotte Circuit. He was anxious to become acquainted with his new neighbor. On his way to a camp meeting in Maryland, within the bounds of the neighboring Oneida Conference, Osborn stopped at Hedstrom's home and invited his new colleague to accompany him to the camp meetings. Hedstrom was timid about doing so since both preachers and people would be total strangers to him. In spite of assurances that he would be warmly received, Hedstrom asked to be excused. Second thoughts dispelled his reticence. To Osborn's pleasant surprise, in the course of a prayer meeting the day after his arrival at the campground, he heard Hedstrom's voice raised in fervent prayer.[7] The warm friendship that developed between these two preachers became personally enriching but also mutually supportive in their common tasks. Joseph Hartwell, writing about Hedstrom, comments: "He and Elbert Osborn were the chief workers in the midsummer revival of 1835 mentioned in the life of Bro. Osborn."[8] Further, since Osborn published an autobiography, he is the source of valuable information concerning Hedstrom not otherwise available.

With the beginning of the Charlotte Circuit, it was recognized that Fergusonville was the principal Methodist Society on the circuit. It was undoubtedly for that reason Hedstrom sought to establish his residence in that community. In succeeding years, it continued to be the place of residence for the circuit preacher. Methodism was deeply rooted in the community. The founder of Fergusonville was James Ferguson, of Scotch-Irish ancestry, who arrived in New York in 1794. Sometime thereafter he migrated to Delaware County, where he settled and reared a family of twelve children. Three of his sons entered the Methodist ministry, and the entire family continued to have close ties to the community that bore their name. Samuel D. Ferguson joined the New York Conference in 1819 and served as a pastor and presiding elder (associate bishop). In the late 1840s, he and his younger brother, Sanford Isaac Ferguson who had been associated with the Methodist Publishing House, founded the Fergusonville Academy, one of a series of New York Conference-related educational institutions established in the Catskill Mountain region.[9]

It is curious to note that though Methodism had existed in the community of Fergusonville for twenty years, meetings were held in homes and possibly in the schoolhouse; there was no church building there when Hedstrom arrived on the circuit. During Hedstrom's first year, a church was built on land donated by Garret Burtis and his wife at a cost of $800 and completed in 1836.[10]

One cannot avoid being impressed by the persons of exceptional quality we discover in Hedstrom's first circuit. The Fergusonville and Charlotteville churches produced unusually capable leadership for both church and community. Among those who entered the ministry were Thomas Lamont, Joseph Hartwell, William S. Stillwell, Nathan T. Shaler, Ezra S. Cook, and Charles Gorse.

At Hedstrom's first quarterly meeting on the Charlotte Circuit, conducted by the presiding elder in Charlotteville on

September 12, 1835, Joseph Hartwell's name was among the applications for a license to preach. Two years earlier, when only sixteen years of age, he had been appointed an exhorter, indicating that he was a young man with religious experience who was endowed with some talent as a speaker. Three years later, in 1838, Joseph Hartwell was received into the Oneida Conference as a probationary member.[11] After several appointments to local churches, Hartwell became financial secretary for Northwestern University. He then established the Society of Church Extension in Chicago and traveled extensively throughout Methodist conferences in various states to promote the organization of similar societies. It is said he raised thousands of dollars, as well as gifts of real property, for churches and parsonages. Further, his influence upon church leadership and in the General Conference of the denomination resulted in the establishment of the Church Extension Society of the Methodist Episcopal Church in 1864.

In his retirement years, Joseph Hartwell wrote a series of articles printed in the *Prattsville District Register*, which he entitled "Chapters from Memory." The seventh chapter was devoted to Olof G. Hedstrom, in which he paid the following significant tribute:

> Rev. O. G. Hedström was a coveted guest at our fireside. He was a grand man physically, socially and spiritually. He was tall, broad shouldered, deep-chested, inured to privations and fatigue. He had a great good heart, full of strong sympathy, and burning with religious zeal. He was ardent in his friendships and exceedingly agreeable in the social circle. He was a man of rapid thought, quick to perceive and prompt to declare the truth.[12]

Recalling the young preacher in his first appointment Hartwell wrote: "A stranger in a strange land, preaching in a language which was foreign to him and living in poverty, that beginning of his work may have seemed to some 'a day of small things,' but his fame was soon noised abroad and he won a multitude of souls for Christ."

Most illuminating is Hartwell's description of Hedstrom's preaching in those early days, revealing both his limitations and his strength in the pulpit. It must have been Hedstrom's first year traveling the Charlotte Circuit that Christmas came on a Sunday. Appropriately, the preacher took for his text, "Glory to God in the highest, on earth peace and good will toward men." Hedstrom was obviously having a hard time preaching. His thoughts circled the text, and he seemed unable to develop a coherent train of thought. His ideas became more and more involved. "Like a fly in a web his efforts only increased his difficulty." Finally, Hedstrom gave up and, leaning over the pulpit, said:

> "Brethren, I had another text on my mind, but as this was Christmas, I thought I must take this, and I have had a hard time." Then he suddenly straightened himself up and with his eyes flashing and his voice sounding like a trumpet, he added, "I will take the other text, 'Except these abide in the ship ye cannot be saved.'" Then came a sermon which enchained our attention. We were soon in the midst of a storm at sea, described so vividly as to seem almost real. This was in the beginning of his ministry. He had just entered the itinerant work, coming from the rocky shores of Sweden a little while before. His mind, though not trained in the culture of the schools, was active, vigorous and clear, and his success was remarkable, both as a preacher and in his pastoral work. As to his preaching it might be said that without a parable spake he not unto them. He was not inclined to metaphysics but his descriptive powers were wonderful. With a text that suggested an army or a ship, a shepherd or a husbandman, he could draw such vivid word pictures as moved even the coldest hearts.

Thomas W. Lamont, well-known financier, philanthropist and chairman of J. P. Morgan and Company, in *My Boyhood in a Parsonage*, gives us information about relatives who would have been known to Hedstrom: the Ferguson family previously mentioned, and the Lamont and Jayne families of the Charlotteville church. His grandfather, Thomas W. Lamont, was the second Methodist class leader at Charlotteville when only sixteen and remained in that office during the remainder of his life. In 1836 he was appointed a member of the Circuit Standing Committee. His son, the Rev. Thomas W. Lamont, married Caroline Jayne, whose father, Walter Peter Jayne, a printer by trade and a master of English composition, had spent some time in Liberia on behalf of the Methodist Episcopal Missionary Society. He edited and published *Africa's Luminary* in Monrovia, an asylum for released or escaped slaves. The first member of the family in America, William Jayne, a Puritan preacher, had come in 1678 and had served as the dominie of the little Setauket, Long Island, Presbyterian church, where he was buried in the church cemetery following his death in 1714. Walter Peter Jayne married one of the Ferguson daughters of Fergusonville.[13] In addition to Thomas Lamont and Joseph Hartwell, the following were exhorters during Hedstrom's tenure and became Methodist preachers: William Stillwell, Nathan T. Shaler, Ezra S. Cook, and Charles Gorse.[14]

Clearly, Hedstrom relished the ambience of revival meetings, and his first year on the circuit was marked by protracted (serial) meetings in his own and neighboring circuits. Hartwell mentions "the mid-summer revival of 1835," of which Olof Hedstrom and Elbert Osborn were the architects. Writing sketchy historical notes concerning the Charlotte Circuit, Edward White comments on an item worthy of special consideration, "In 1835, under the labors of Olif [*sic*] G. Hedstrom, there was a gracious revival all through the circuit."[15]

Sometime in July, only two months after Hedstrom's arrival on the circuit, he announced a revival to be held in the northern part of Davenport on the Charlotte Circuit. Presumably the little group of Methodists, probably a class not yet organized as a church, had been meeting in a home or some other limited facility. Arrangements were made to hold the protracted meetings in a barn large enough to accommodate the anticipated congregation. In accordance with prevailing custom, support and assistance from neighboring circuit preachers were solicited. Hedstrom invited his new friend Elbert Osborn, his colleague on the Jefferson Circuit John Bangs, and D. Sparks from another circuit. Their participation in preaching, exhortation, and prayer enhanced the significance of the revival meetings. The event attracted attention, and the duration of the daily meetings depended upon interest and response, with some lasting for several weeks. Though the barn was aesthetically and ecclesiastically barren, Osborn found it symbolically significant: "The blessed Redeemer, who was once cradled in the manger, condescended to meet with us in much mercy in the barn, and several were converted to God."[16]

Elbert Osborn was at his home on August 3 when a messenger arrived from Charlotteville with the good news that "God had begun a gracious work there," and his assistance was desired. Two sermons, one by Hedstrom and the other by Calvin Hawley of the Westford Circuit in the adjoining Oneida Conference, had "produced powerful effects." Hawley was unable to remain longer because of duties on his own circuit, so Osborn took his place. He later related the impact that the revival had upon the Charlotteville community.[17]

Another quarterly meeting of which we have knowledge on the Charlotte Circuit was held December 12 and 13, 1835. It was very definitely held to gain converts at that preaching point. This was Hedstrom's first year (and if the schedule was kept, would have been Hedstrom's second such meeting).

Osborn has the following account: "On the 12th and 13th of December 1835, a quarterly meeting was held in the lower part of Davenport, in Mr. Hedstrom's circuit. It was held in a building which had been occupied in the business of tanning and currying leather. Of course it was not a very pleasant place for a large worshipping assembly. But I suppose it was the best that could be then obtained in the neighborhood."[18]

When Hedstrom started revival meetings on his own circuit, he was the beneficiary of ministerial assistance from beyond his circuit boundaries. He gladly reciprocated when called upon. During the first months of his circuit ministry, Hedstrom responded to two opportunities to participate in programs first at Summit Four Corners and then at Eminence, both in the Jefferson Circuit. About the first Osborn noted, "On the next day (Thursday) another dear brother, who had also been with us at Charlotteville, came to our help. He was brother Hedstrom."

A series of revival meetings began November 17 in Eminence, a hamlet that had been known as Dutch Hill, since prominent among its settlers were families of Dutch and German ancestry. A service was well under way when Hedstrom arrived one evening. A complete stranger to the congregation, Hedstrom was invited by Osborn to provide an exhortation at the conclusion of the sermon. He began, "I have just been thinking that if such a sermon as we have just heard could be preached to my countrymen on the rocky shores of Sweden, what multitudes would turn to the Lord." No other words were necessary. Osborn wrote: "The foreign accent of the stranger, and the deep feeling manifest in the intonation of his voice, instantly attracted the attention of the whole congregation; and scarcely had he uttered the short sentence which I have just quoted, before it seemed that nearly every one in the house was melted into tears."[19]

Osborn soon found a way of exploiting beneficially Hedstrom's colorful life experiences and his talent for word pictures. Hedstrom was invited to preach an autobiographical sermon before several congregations:

It was very interesting to listen to his description of the moral darkness which surrounded him in Sweden, the land of his birth; and of his feeling after his arrival here, as he contrasted the civil and religious liberty of this happy land with what he had seen in the old world. But when he spoke of his conviction of sin, and his first draught from the well of salvation; . . .

when he told us of his visit to his native land, and his interview with his aged father, after an absence of many years, and the effect which his testimony for God had, through the divine blessing, upon his father and other friends, the hearts of almost all who heard him seemed to be deeply affected.[20]

It must be recognized that both Hartwell and Osborn wrote about Hedstrom in their later years, long after he had attained worldwide recognition for his work on the Bethel Ship in New York Harbor. Their recollections were bound to be colored by the totality of his well-publicized ministry. However, these recollections of his earliest ministry, their appraisal of his work as a circuit preacher, and their insights into his nature and personal characteristics point to a charismatic quality in Hedstrom as well as a genuine piety and integrity.

We have another specific reference to a sermon preached by Hedstrom during his Catskill Mountain ministry approximately six years later. He had been appointed the second preacher on the Windham Circuit. Daniel Steele, a theological professor at Boston University School of Theology, recalls the ministry of Olof Hedstrom on the Windham Circuit, of which he and his family had been active members:

> In his preaching [Hedstrom] displayed extraordinary seriousness. No person ever doubted the sincerity and genuineness of his conversion. He had a burning zeal for souls which overcame all indifference and resistance. Those who came to criticize his broken English, often remained to pray. His warm-heartedness and sympathy substantially increased the effectiveness of his sermons. Some of these I still retain in vivid remembrance although heard half a century ago. On the text: "How shall we escape if we neglect so great a salvation" his points were as follows:
>
> 1. There is no escape from the call to judgement.
> 2. The Court never adjourns.
> 3. Clever lawyers cannot evade the law.
> 4. The Judge cannot be bribed.[21]

Steele's recollections also pay tribute to Hedstrom's pastoral work and to his warm, personal relations. Hedstrom lived in a house that was owned by Steele's father, and was their nearest neighbor. Because of his imperfect knowledge of written English, Hedstrom called upon young Daniel to serve as a secretary, particularly in writing reports of his revivals, which was frequent since, according to Steele, "his preaching was in spirit and power."

The circuit was large, embracing eighteen preaching places, mostly in schoolhouses in the Windham-Lexington-Hunter districts of the Catskill Mountains. Shortly after Hedstrom's arrival in Windham in April 1841, he invited Daniel to accompany him to his next place of preaching, with the purpose, says Steele, "of inviting me in the most gentle fashion, to come to Christ." During one such journey, Hedstrom informed his young friend that "he predicted that before he left the circuit he would see me 'Happy in God's love.'"

In the winter of 1841–42, Daniel Steele began his first attempt to teach school in Hunter. The schoolhouse was next door to the Methodist church. The "untiring Swede," as Steele called him, came to this church to hold a series of meetings: "I do not know how many were converted at these, but I do know that the young school teacher began to pray in his school, and also to confess his need of Christ, and further he began to receive intimations of his future life work which led him to enroll in Wesleyan Seminary at Wilbraham. It was here he entered more fully into 'the glorious freedom of God's children.'"[22]

Thus were the seeds sown that flowered in Steele's fifty-one-year active ministerial career, almost equally divided between pastorates in the New England Conference and academic work at Wesleyan University, Genesee College, Syracuse University (for a while as acting president), and Boston University, where he taught New Testament Greek, systematic theology, and practical theology. In addition, Steele was a widely read author. He was to visit with Hedstrom on two occasions, once when he called on him at the Bethel Ship and heard about the important and successful service being rendered. Later, he met his friend in Lynn, Massachusetts, at a missionary conference, when Hedstrom was a speaker. Sixty years after the fact, Steele could still recall his early impression of Hedstrom:

> . . . I can see him in my mind's eye—a well-built and manly person, thirty-five years of age, about six feet in height, with clear and healthy complexion and a well-shaped head covered with thick wavy hair, black as a raven's wing. I can still see him in the little red school in the Catskill Mountains, admonishing with holy earnestness the sinners to be reconciled with God. Again, I see him by the door of the parsonage, saddling his horse, preparing to depart for his three-week circuit. His wife draws a bucket of water for the horse. He mounts and says, "Come Car'line and open the gate." His devoted wife trips forward to the gate, and away 'rides salvation's messenger, happier than a king.[23]

In this chapter we have explored the early ministry of Olof Hedstrom. We have seen a person of considerable ability and great dedication overcome the limitation of language and lack of academic training. His more scholarly peers applauded his effectiveness and cherished his friendship.

The work for which he became renowned in his own day and is remembered today lay ahead on the Bethel Ship in New York Harbor, chiefly among Scandinavian sailors and immigrants. Before moving to that aspect of our story, we need to consider the religious life of Sweden and a movement that under varying names arose among several nations of Europe in the eighteenth and nineteenth centuries.

4

Hedstrom's Relation to the Läsare

The term *läsare* is peculiar to the Swedish language. Applied
first in derision to a small group of Christian pietists meeting in
the province of Västergötland, Sweden, in the 1750s, the name
remained in common usage for over 150 years and was applied
to all piestitically minded groups and individuals of various
persuasions.[1] Almost any person who took his or her religion
with unusual seriousness could expect to be called a *läsare*.

The Västergötland group met in private homes for Bible
reading, prayer, and conversation about spiritual matters.
They also evaluated pastors of the churches in the area and
searched out those they regarded as "awakened," those for
whom religion was an inner personal matter rather than
outward form. They performed these activities in spite of a
law enacted in 1726 prohibiting religious gatherings not
authorized by the established Church of Sweden.

The *läsare* in Västergötland were by no means the first or
only such group in Sweden at this time. German pietism had
been introduced into Sweden in the 1720s. Soon, small groups
of pietists began to dot certain areas of the Swedish landscape.
Ernst Newman states, "During the latter half of the eighteenth
century . . . the basic principles of pietism began increasingly to penetrate folk life . . . and everywhere one encountered the ferment of *Herrnhut* [i.e., Moravian] influences."[2]

We must not think of the *läsare* movement in isolation. F.
Ernest Stoeffler has placed pietism in its wider Continental
context.

The importance of the rise of Pietism for the Protestant
experience in general has only recently begun to dawn upon

us. In the grip of Orthodoxy both the Reform and the Lutheran churches on the Continent had often lost touch with the vital concerns of religion, concentrating their efforts on the attempt to answer questions which were no longer being asked, and to solve problems which were widely felt to bear little relationship to man's workaday experience. Under the circumstances large numbers of nominal Protestants treated their churches with benign neglect, respectfully accepting them as institutions to which one turns to be baptized, married, and buried, but which should not be expected to enter vitally into life's concerns.

Not until the advent of Pietism did this state of affairs begin to change significantly. During much of the seventeenth century, and throughout the eighteenth, it engendered a new spirit of religious devotion. . . . Religious faith began to be regarded as a live option by large segments of the population which had hitherto thought of it as little more than a cultural relic.[3]

Among the results, as noted by Stoeffler, was a religious orientation toward one's individual and corporate needs. Preaching and pastoral work were revitalized and a new hymnody came into existence. A fresh vision of responsibility to the community and the nation was engendered, with Christians becoming more sensitive to the needs of the disadvantaged, the sick, and the dying. Bible study required reading skills, and so the movement formed educational institutions of all sorts. For the first time in Protestant history, Christians began to think seriously of a worldwide witness to its faith in word and deed. It is no accident that the golden age of Christian missions would mark the churches in the next century.

There were various forms of Continental pietism. While they had a common thrust, each was conditioned by the theological and social milieu in which it evolved. Each was also impressed by the peculiar qualities and character of its leadership. Two of the forms clearly identified are Moravianism in Germany and Wesleyan Methodism in England. Both found their way into Sweden and became determining elements in fashioning the *läsare* movement.

The *läsare* expression of pietism has been intensively studied by Swedish scholars and church historians. Two recognized authorities are Gunnar Westin of Uppsala University and Ernst Newman of Lund University. It is significant that both men, writing in different contexts, define the movement with the hyphenated phrase *Herrnhutisk-Metodistiska*.[4] Though there was interaction between the two, there were also distinct and peculiar differences. Through the *läsare* they exerted a widespread, transforming influence on Swedish religious life, characterized by George M. Stephenson as "a second religious reformation in Sweden."[5]

In light of the purpose of this study, several questions require answers. What was the nature of the movement that could be captioned *Herrnhutisk-Metodistiska* and that had influenced a substantial number of the immigrants from Sweden? How had these two foreign influences pervaded Swedish religious life? What role did Hedstrom play in the Methodist branch of the movement through his work with immigrants on the Bethel Ship?

In response to the questions, we shall deal briefly with each of the two basic elements in the Swedish context. To interpret the impact of Methodism on Swedish religious life, we are compelled to consider three dynamic characters—Carl Magnus Wrangel, George Scott, and Olof Gustaf Hedstrom. Their contributions were made at three points in the *läsare* movement.

Philipp Jakob Spener, regarded as the founder of German pietism, wrote his *Pia Desideria* in 1675, which provided a platform for his movement. However simple it might seem to us, in the eyes of the established Lutheran church, it was radical. The six "desideria" were:

1. Bible study in small groups, called conventicles.
2. Restoration of the priesthood of all believers.
3. Practice of Christian principles in daily life.
4. Love instead of argument in dealing with dissenters and unbelievers.

5. Reform of theological education to emphasize personal religion.
6. Deeper spirituality in preaching—a return to apostolic simplicity and sincerity.[6]

Spener was godfather to Count Nicholas Zinzendorf, who was destined to become Spener's successor. At the age of ten he was sent to the school at Halle established by Spener's associate, August Herman Francke. After university training at Wittenberg, Zinzendorf conceived the idea of a Christian association, the members of which would seek to awaken a dormant church through preaching, writing, traveling, and works of charity.

Zinzendorf's dream became a reality in 1722 when a group of Christian refugees arrived in Germany from Moravia. They were adherents of the principles taught by John Huss and were seeking to escape religious persecution. Zinzendorf gave them asylum on his Berthelsdorf estate and there established the Herrnhut (the Lord's safekeeping) community. In collaboration with the Moravian pietists, the movement became international in scope and missionary in spirit.

Even before Herrnhut, an older form of German pietism had been introduced into Sweden by German students engaged by wealthy families of southern Sweden as tutors for their children. Two such young men were Johan Werner Pause and Johan Schade, who had been influenced by the writing of Johan Arndt. A more radical pietism, however, came as a result of the Northern War. Hilding Pleijel describes the consequences of the war on the religious life of Sweden:

> It was quite different when the Karolingian captives of war returned to the homeland immediately before and after the peace in 1721. During the long and difficult years of captivity many a soldier had found comfort in the Bible and Psalm book [i.e., hymnal], and also in the writing of Arndt, Spener and Francke. A number had united with the "Collegia Pietatis." A small group had even entered into correspondence

with Francke. After their arrival home, these Karolingians often became devoted pioneers for Pietism, and many states, even in Scania, became havens of refuge for the devotees of Pietism.[7]

Some pastors encouraged the growing movement. The established Church of Sweden, supported by the majority of its clergy, was in opposition. Fearing that private meetings, unrelated to the Church, were a threat to its authority and could easily lead to theological heresy, the Konventikelplakat (Conventicle Edict) was enacted in 1726 to prevent such gatherings. Further, the fourteenth article of the Lutheran Augsburg Confession was applied. This document proclaimed that only those regularly called by the Church could teach religion publicly. Although penalties were prescribed for violations, efforts to restrain the growth of the movement failed.[8] The prohibition against conventicles remained in force until 1858.

A brief account of John Wesley's spiritual odyssey seems imperative if we are to understand Methodism's contribution to the *läsare* movement defined as *Herrnhutisk-Metodistiska*. The movement began in the middle 1720s with the Holy Club at Oxford, where Wesley was a don. Here, he and a few like-minded young people were responding to the moral and spiritual malaise in the English church and society of that day. The young men took their religion seriously and were so disciplined in prayer, Bible study, and acts of charity that, in derision, they were dubbed Methodists—even as their Swedish counterparts were called *läsare*.

Acknowledging this account to be an oversimplification, five elements of the odyssey are as follows:

1. John Wesley, an ordained clergyman of the Church of England, believed that the sacraments of the Church were a means of grace, and though conscious of his spiritual deficiencies, could lead toward salvation. In contrast, Herrnhut pietism reserved communion only for those who had an assurance of salvation. Wesley accepted the Anglican church's

Thirty-nine Articles of faith. When American Methodism separated from the parent body in England, Wesley chose twenty-five of the Articles that he considered most important to be the creedal foundation for the American church.

2. John and Charles Wesley came from a family of Puritan dissenters and nonconformists. This was true of both sides of the family; their mother, whose influence on them is well documented, was the daughter of a prominent London nonconformist preacher.[9]

3. John Wesley was a student of the early church fathers and also of the more contemporary mystics. They shaped much of his religious thought. He acknowledged his indebtedness to Jeremy Taylor's *Rule and Exercises of Holy Living and Dying*; Thomas à Kempis's *Christian Pattern*; and William Law's *Christian Perfection* and *Serious Call*. Stimulated by them, Wesley developed his concept of Christian perfection, which he came to believe was his most significant contribution to Methodist theology. He was under constant pressure to explain, interpret, and defend the principle, which was distorted by friend and foe alike. He believed that God provided forgiveness of sins, but also power to overcome and conquer sin. Christian perfection is a process rather than an achieved state—the goal toward which the Christian strives. In the words of Albert C. Outler, a leading Wesleyan theologian, "Thus, the gift of perfection is to be sought and expected—but never scheduled or advertised."[10]

4. The Moravian influence was crucial in the lives of both John and Charles Wesley. They had become acquainted with Moravians during a missionary journey to Georgia in 1735–37. Returning to London, John Wesley went to a Moravian meeting house on Aldersgate Street on the evening of May 24, 1738. During the reading of Luther's preface to the Epistle to the Romans, in which Luther defines the meaning of faith as the sole factor in justification, Wesley experienced a great change. "About a quarter before nine, while he was describing the change which God works in the heart through faith in Christ, I felt my heart strangely warmed. I felt I did

trust in Christ, Christ alone, for salvation; and an assurance was given to me that He had taken away my sins, even mine, and saved me from the law of sin and death."[11]

Prior to this experience, Wesley's religion had been intellectual and ethical, a burdensome, personal striving with rigid discipline which left him dissatisfied. It had now become an inward experiential power.

5. On an October day that year, while walking from London to Oxford, Wesley read a narrative account by Jonathan Edwards describing conversions taking place in North Hampton in New England. Of this event Outler says, "It is an arresting and moving account, and it struck Wesley with terrific force. The crisis which followed ranks with Aldersgate in importance if not in drama. . . . It is not too much to say that one of the effectual causes of the Wesleyan Revival in England was the Great Awakening in New England."[12]

Wesley adopted Edwards's criteria of "the distinguishing marks of a work of the Spirit of God." He published an abridgment of *A Treatise Concerning the Religious Affections*, in which Edwards contends that "he that had doctrinal knowledge and speculation only, without affection, never is engaged in the business of religion. . . . True religion is a powerful thing . . . a ferment, a vigorous engagedness of the heart."[13]

We have sought in capsule form to delineate the essential details of German Herrnhutism and English Wesleyan Methodism. With reference to the former, we have also seen how it was introduced into Sweden's religious life. Further, we have noted the efforts of the established Church to control and, if possible, eliminate what it perceived to be an insidious and divisive threat to Church discipline and Lutheran orthodoxy.

It is now necessary to trace the avenues and accidents of history by which John Wesley's Methodism came to Sweden in the eighteenth century and in the nineteenth century became identified with and provided leadership for the *läsare* movement. Indeed, Gunnar Westin states that the terms *läsare* and Methodist were practically interchangeable by 1840.

The first contact Sweden had with Methodism occurred in the latter half of the eighteenth century. Several Swedish churchmen and scholars had been sufficiently intrigued with the work of John Wesley in England to have traveled there and become personally acquainted with him. Johan Henrik Liden, a history professor at Lund University, attended Wesley's services at Spitalfields and Foundery in London on October 15, 1769. In true scholarly fashion, he formulated a series of questions concerning the nature, structure, and strength of Methodism. These were answered by Wesley in a communication dated November 16, 1769.[14] A noted bibliophile, Liden assembled a complete collection of Wesley's published writings which ultimately found their way into diocesan and university libraries. When Carl Magnus Wrangel arrived in Gothenburg after a visit with Wesley, he discovered that his host, Bishop Lambert of the Gothenburg Diocese, regarded Wesley as a friend.[15] N. S. Swederus, pastor at Näsby and Ervalla, visited England in 1784–85 and became well acquainted with John Wesley.[16] He cherished an autographed volume of Wesley's writing.

Sweden decided to join other European nations in colonizing America. The first Swedes arrived on the *Kalmar Nyckel* (the Key of Kalmar) in 1638 and built Fort Christina near the mouth of the Delaware River, now Wilmington. Over the next few years, Swedish communities were settled along the Delaware Valley as far north as Philadelphia and Swedesboro, New Jersey. Swedish control did not last long. In 1655, the Dutch took over civil administration, to be followed by the British in 1684. However, the churches established in the several communities continued their relationship with the Church of Sweden and were known by it as the American mission. Between 1831 and 1858, the churches described in resolutions as the United Swedish Lutheran Churches were transferred to the Protestant Episcopal Church in America. Though Lutheran in its faith, the Church of Sweden is Episcopal in its church polity.

The most significant contact between Sweden and John

Wesley in the eighteenth century came through the afore-
mentioned Carl Magnus Wrangel. Historians have recognized him as the first to bring a Wesleyan impact upon
Swedish religious life. Wrangel was born in 1717, the son of an
aristocratic family, Wrangel of Sag and Wachel. After taking a
graduate degree in Germany and receiving Lutheran ordination in Strängnäs, he was appointed dean of the American
mission in 1758. He became pastor of Gloria Dei church in
Philadelphia.[17]

Wrangel remained at this post for nine productive years.
His biographer describes him as "a revivalist preacher with a
strain of pietism." He was popular and influential in the
religious life of the Delaware Valley beyond the Swedish
churches under his care. When George Whitefield, an associate of John Wesley, won some converts in the Philadelphia
area on an itinerant visit, Wrangel provided encouragement
to them and invited Captain Thomas Webb from New York to
give pastoral oversight. The nineteenth-century Methodist
historian Abel Stevens designates Webb the founder of Methodism in Philadelphia, but he cannot forget the contribuion
of the Swede, Dr. C. M. Wrangel: "The zealous and catholic
doctor had been preparing the way for Methodism in Philadelphia."

It is not surprising that when, in 1768, Wrangel returned to
Sweden, he stopped off in Bristol, England, to meet John
Wesley and made an urgent appeal for the need of Methodist
preachers in America. John Wesley's journal contains two
references to this visit:

> Fri. 14 [October 1768] I dined with Dr. Wrangel, one of the
> King of Sweden's chaplains, who has spent several years in
> Pennsylvania. His heart seemed to be greatly united to the
> American Christians, and he strongly pleaded for our send-
> ing some of our preachers to help them, multitudes of whom
> are as sheep without a shepherd.
> Tues. 18, He preached at the New Room [a Methodist
> meeting house in Bristol] to a crowded audience, and gave

general satisfaction by the simplicity and life which accompanied his sound doctrine.[18]

Wrangel maintained communication through correspondence with Wesley for several years. Back in Sweden, Wrangel designed a plan for a religious society within the Lutheran church not unlike Wesley's connection of Methodist societies within the Church of England. He became a court chaplain and used the place of prominence which he attained within the church to further his ideas. In a letter to Wesley dated May 5, 1770, Wrangel wrote, "Last Parliament session several clergymen, including four Bishops, agreed to my proposal concerning a Society for Propagating Practical Religion."

The society was called *Pro Fide et Christianismo.* It had at least a quasi-official relationship to the established Church of Sweden. John Wesley accepted an invitation to become a corresponding member of the society, and in his letter pledged to do all in his power to forward the society's designs. One of the first proposed activities was a mission to the Laplanders. Wesley expressed both amazement and admiration because of the low estimation in which Laplanders were regarded in England. Another activity was the establishment of a society library, a substantial part of which consisted of Wesleyan publications.

The ultimate goal of the society was undoubtedly renewal of the Church of Sweden and evangelization of the general population, as is evident in its Lapp mission. However, the Latin title of the society would indicate an organization of clergymen and the well-educated. This is confirmed in a letter from John Wesley, written four years after his membership: "One thing, gentlemen, I am particularly surprised in the account of the Society with which you favor me—that in Sweden men of rank, of quality, of eminence are not ashamed of the Gospel of Christ; are not ashamed openly to espouse His cause and to give public testimony that they believe the Bible."[19] There is no evidence that *Pro Fide et Christianismo* had any profound influence upon the common people of Sweden. Moravianism continued as the dominant pietistic influence at work among the general population. Wesleyan Methodism and its founder did, however, gain a place of respect and admiration among a segment of the clergy who understood what his movement had accomplished in England. This sympathetic appreciation undoubtedly made possible a wider acceptance of Methodism when it was introduced a second time almost fifty years later.

Much more significant in the history of Sweden's religious life was the direct introduction of Methodism, which began in 1827 with the establishment of an English chapel in the heart of the capital city of Stockholm. Its origins can be traced to a mercantile venture. A member of the Swedish chancellery, A. N. Edelcrantz, purchased four steam engines from Leeds, England. He required an engineer to set them up and train personnel for their operation. The task fell to Samuel Owen, who made extended visits to Sweden from 1804 to 1806. Encouraged by friends who recognized his potential value to Swedish industry, Owen returned in 1809 and established his own foundry on Skeppsholmen in Stockholm, where he began to build steamships. He soon became a prominent and honored member of the Stockholm community—elected to the Academy of Science and knighted by the king of Sweden. A bronze plaque later fastened to the wall of the foundry building named Owen "founding father of Sweden's steam powered navy and the foundry industry."[20]

Unable to secure employees with the required industrial skills, Owen brought a complement of workers and their families from his homeland, thus creating an English colony in Stockholm. Converted through preaching before coming to Sweden, some of his English workers were probably Methodists. In 1825, Owen made a return trip to England and during his stay renewed his Methodist contacts. He was apparently dissatisfied with the spiritual sterility within the established Church of Sweden and the moral ambience of Stockholm, including rampant alcohol abuse. Owen was concerned for the spiritual welfare of his own growing family but also felt some responsibility toward his workers and their families. He approached the Methodist Missionary Society with a request that a missionary be sent to Stockholm, and in July of 1826 Joseph R. Stephens arrived.[21] Stephens was an ideal choice as a first pastor of the English chapel. He established a good foundation for its work and related well to the various segments of the population attracted to the chapel, including the British and American legations personnel. Beyond that, he ingratiated himself with Swedish authorities and the better-educated portion of the Swedish population. The program developed well from the beginning in the new chapel, which was a converted summer garden pavilion at the home of Count Carl de Geer, well-situated near Stora Trädgårdsgatan. The chapel, with a seating capacity of from two hundred to three hundred persons, was opened December 3, 1826.[22] Stephens was, in the words of Gunnar Westin, a "Väckelse Predikant"—a revival preacher whose chief aim was religious awakening. He attracted attention and response. A gifted linguist, Stephens soon learned Swedish and enlarged his ministry by holding services in that language—though not in such a way as to interfere with regular church schedules. He remained in Sweden only three years.

George Scott was sent to Sweden in 1830 as Stephens's replacement by the Wesleyan Methodist Missionary Society. He came at a propitious moment in Swedish religious history. Rationalism pervaded most of the Stockholm pulpits. Herrnhut pietism, though widely spread in certain areas of the country, had never gained a stronghold in the capital city. There it had declined almost to the vanishing point. Furthermore, the *läsare* movement throughout Sweden seemed to be listlessly drifting with no recognized leader to give it direction. In writing of this period, Westin observes, "The *läsare* movement needed a gifted leader, preferably in the capital city of the Kingdom, and in addition it needed the publication of a periodical. Both of these needs were satisfied in the 1830's."[23]

Scott became that aggressive and dynamic leader. *Pietisten*, the journal he founded in January 1942 and funded with an annual stipend from American sources, became the most widely read religious periodical in Sweden. Through Scott's leadership the *läsare*, as a pietistic dissenting movement, were significantly revitalized through the infusion of the Methodist spirit and emphasis. So great was the transformation that at the close of the decade "*läsare*" and "Methodism" were practically synonymous.[24] George M. Stephenson pays high tribute to this leader:

> Scott's great contribution was the impulse he gave to a moral renaissance in Sweden through the organization of temperance societies, through addresses and publications, and through the torch of his inspiration to a healthier religious practice—a torch throwing its rays into spiritual darkness—which he handed down to men and women who consecrated themselves to serve among their countrymen in Sweden and America.[25]

Scott became the instrument through which Anglo-American ideas and methods of religious work were introduced into Sweden. He also was a typical Methodist revival preacher. His services in both English and Swedish at the chapel attracted an increasingly larger number of attendants, making the building of a new edifice imperative.

There were some theological distinctions between the Moravians and the Methodists in England that caused a separation. However, Arthur Wilford Nagler, in his *Pietism and Methodism*, has undoubtedly identified one of the greatest differences in terms of national culture and temperament: "The difference may be variously interpreted. In the first place, national characteristics played an important role in the development of both movements. The expansive activity of the Englishman would lead to different results from those due to the intensive activity of the German."[26] This comment is also germane to the role of Methodism and the *läsare* movement in Sweden.

In Sweden, the Anglo-American concept of organizing societies, each to advance a specific cause, was placed in practice. Missions, temperance, Sunday and infant schools, Bible and tract distribution—all were promoted through the development of appropriate societies. Though Scott was the instigator, the societies were developed independently of the English chapel. Strategically, the concept of independent societies was both practical and useful. It made it possible to secure cooperation and leadership from sympathetic Lutheran pastors and laypersons within the established church. The Temperance Society became a powerful instrument in the service of that cause. Among its leaders were Peter Wieselgren and Lars P. Esbjörn, both prominent pastors who were identified as *läsare* pastors. The society had the patronage of the royal house. The service and talents of laypersons, underutilized by the Church of Sweden, found meaningful expression as colporteurs, teachers, and social workers.

Scott's trip to America in 1841 to raise funds for his Stockholm mission had both positive and negative results.[27] On the positive side, he secured funds from American church agencies and individuals, which guaranteed the continuation of his work even after it became necessary for Scott to leave Sweden. During his absence from Sweden, Scott placed Carl O. Rosenius, a *läsare* pastor's *läsare* son, in charge of the program. The young man was brilliant, articulate, and deeply committed. He had been associated with Scott for some time and was sympathetic to the ideas and the methods of his mentor. Consequently, there was a tested apprenticed leader in place to continue the movement and even expand its influence. Westin insisted that Scott's greatest conquest was Carl O. Rosenius.[28]

Scott and Hedstrom became acquainted when both were present at the New York Annual Conference of the Methodist Episcopal Church on May 21, 1841. Eight years earlier, in 1833, both had been within a relatively short distance of one another. Scott was at work in Stockholm and Hedstrom in southeastern Sweden. Both Methodists had been similarly engaged in the *läsare* interests, though Hedstrom in a limited fashion, mostly with relatives and friends. Did Hedstrom hear about Scott and his work in Stockholm? We do not know. It is doubtful that Scott could have heard of Hedstrom's private efforts. When they did meet, the question of how Hedstrom might be useful in the Swedish mission came quickly to Scott's mind. In less than a month, a plan had been formalized and clearances secured. The following three diary entries tell the story.

> May 21. Met a dear Br. [Hedstrom] a Swede, who has been travelling preacher in this Conference for 8 years, a good and zealous man, and ardently desirous of advancing the interests of his country.
>
> May 25. Made my proposition that Br. Hedstrom might be supported in a visit to Sweden next Spring, to see what the Providence of God would open for him to do; this was well received, and Dr. H. Spoke on the subject in a manner that melted all to tears.
>
> June 16. At the meeting of the Meth. Missionary Board. Got a promise that Hedstrom should be sent out next Spring, at the expense of the Board, on a visit to Sweden.[29]

Two days later, June 18, 1841, Scott wrote a letter to the Committee of the Wesleyan Methodist Missionary Society in London, which included the following statement:

> The Methodist Missionary Board has agreed to bear the expense of a visit to be made next year to his friends in Sweden, of a Preacher in the New York Conference, who is a native of that country, and could, I have no doubt, be usefully employed in his own land, though till I converse with the Archbishop I am not prepared to say in what way.[30]

During the next three months, Scott traveled among churches and church agencies in America, planting seeds that provided an important harvest of financial and spiritual support for the Stockholm mission. As matters developed, that support became a crucial factor in securing its future. Unwittingly, Scott had also sown seeds that sprouted on Swedish soil in the form of thorny thistles, to which we shall later return. On September 30, Scott boarded a vessel for his return trip to Sweden. Before it sailed, he fulfilled one final obligation that testifies to the importance he placed on negotiations regarding Hedstrom. He wrote a letter to Dr. Charles Pitman, secretary of the Missionary Society of the Methodist Episcopal Church.

On Board the Narragansett
September 30, 1841

Dear Brother:

Lest the statement I made regarding Brother Hedstrom's projected visit to Sweden should have, in the multiplicity of your onerous duties, escaped your mind, I make it my last employment in leaving New York, to repeat it in this form, feeling assured it will receive that degree of attention from you and the Board of Missions which it may be found to deserve. I understand, of course, that, according to the decision of the Board, Hedstrom is to come to Sweden next spring, and having had frequent opportunities of knowing his devout wish to benefit his native land, and in listening to his ardent appeals for Sweden, I felt that could he be liberated from his circuit for some months previous to his setting out; and allowed to visit several Methodist Societies, to talk to the churches about Sweden, his intended mission there, he might not only obtain by collection and subscriptions what might be requisite for the expense of his journey, but what is perhaps of more consequence in the future aspect of the enterprise, secure the sympathies and prayers of numerous Christians in his work and labor of love. It would be well if he could be in Sweden early in the year 1842, say before the end of April, though his voyage over would be more pleasant in May, and if he reached his native soil by the close of that month he would have good opportunity of ascertaining what his future course ought to be. I need not say how heartily and gratefully I shall welcome this beloved brother, or how readily I shall exert what little influence I may possess to promote his benevolent purposes. Please present to the Board my respectful and most affectionate regards, and believe me, dear brother, yours in love unfeigned,

Geo. Scott[31]

There can be little doubt that Hedstrom entered into the proposed plan for a second missionary journey to Sweden with some enthusiasm. The communications imply that Scott and Hedstrom had, on various occasions, considered together ways in which the latter could prove useful to the Methodist cause. However, a plan did not materialize, and the reason is easily surmised. While seeking American support, Scott portrayed the moral and spiritual conditions in Sweden in dismal terms—this he could do without exaggeration. Many who participated in the spiritual awakening in Sweden would certainly verify Scott's testimony. Possibly he should have been more sensitive to Swedish reaction. The *läsare* movement, as would be expected, had its natural opponents among both clergy and laypeople. Scott, the recognized leader, was a natural target for the opposition. Statements by Scott were reported in the press. After his return home, the furor became increasingly violent to the point where, on Palm Sunday in 1842, Scott was driven from the church and was compelled to leave Sweden in danger of physical harm.[32] Years later, Scott was to return to Sweden for a visit and was warmly received. He was awarded elaborate accolades and invited to preach in important Church of Sweden pulpits.[33]

Denied an opportunity for a second missionary journey to Sweden, almost exactly four years after Scott had conceived a plan involving his collaboration with the Stockholm mission, Hedstrom, through circumstances we have previously described, was at work among the same constituency under changed circumstances in his adopted country. In many ways his ministry to the arriving immigrant was far more significant and enduring. After the trauma of a long and difficult ocean voyage and facing the uncertainties of a strange land, there was a poignant urgency in their need for spiritual comfort and assurance, as well as the welcome of a helpful friend. Many of these who could resist the *läsare* appeal in Sweden were far more susceptible to the spiritual ministry offered in the Bethel Ship.

Historically, one must conclude that Hedstrom's Bethel Ship work was a continuation and extension of Scott's work, now under the direction of Rosenius and his colleagues in Sweden. The spirit of both had strong similarities. Those who became familiar with the structure and emphasis of the English chapel in Stockholm, with its class meetings, Sunday school, and its revival preaching, discovered that the program on the Bethel Ship was not very different. Scott and Hedstrom shared a common Anglo-American Methodist religious ambience.

The Swedish immigrant churches as they developed on American soil reflected what Stephenson has called the "second religious reformation in Sweden." This was as true of the Lutheran church as of the so-called free churches. As Stephenson states, "Of still more importance to the student of immigration is the fact that the men who laid the foundations of the Swedish Lutheran Church in America were *läsare* pastors and laymen whose lives were shaped by *läsare* pastors."[34]

It is generally recognized that Scott, though a Methodist, did not establish institutional Methodism in Sweden. The Augustana Synod of the Lutheran Church in America was the product of Scott's work among the people of Sweden. He was its progenitor. And he was, in a general way, the progenitor of the free church movement in Sweden. Lars P. Esbjörn, the first Swedish-American Lutheran pastor, was proud to be identified as a *läsare* pastor. Swedish Methodism on both sides of the Atlantic, as we shall note in the next chapter, was the product of Hedstrom's work on the Bethel Ship.

5

Peter Bergner, Pioneer Missionary

The Bethel Ship, a floating chapel in New York Harbor, and its pastor, the Reverend Olof Gustaf Hedstrom, are well known to students of nineteenth-century immigration. Not so well known is Peter Bergner. In all probability there would never have been a Bethel Ship were it not for Bergner. The catalyst for the entire project, he inaugurated the first Swedish-language service ever to be held in the city of New York, and quite likely the first in America outside of the old Swedish colonies on the Delaware. He played a crucial role in persuading a reluctant Olof Hedstrom to come to New York as a missionary pastor to Swedish seamen and to the early beginnings of a burgeoning Swedish immigrant population. However, to historians spanning several decades of accomplishment, Peter Bergner has been eclipsed by the towering figure of Olof Hedstrom. Contemporary observers were inclined to speak appreciatively of Bergner's significant contribution. Typical of the articles appearing in religious periodicals of the time was a concluding comment by a correspondent to the *Missionary Advocate* in its May 1846 issue, describing Bergner's conversion: "You have here the conversion of a sailor, to whom perhaps more than to any other man, the present services of the 'Bethel Ship' owe their origin."[1]

The long-term consequences of the Bethel Ship program are beyond calculation, considering the religious and humanitarian services rendered to thousands of immigrants—travel-weary, apprehensive, often lonely and homesick, confused in a new environment amid unfamiliar customs, frustrated by their inability to communicate, sometimes destitute.[2] Coming from a land astir with a religious ferment characterized by personal pietism, how grateful they must have been for the spiritual comfort and assurance they received in their native language both in personal counsel and public worship on the Bethel Ship. One can well imagine the immigrants' response when sailing into the port of New York to find a moored floating chapel flying the Swedish flag, together with the Bethel Ship banner indicating that it was a "house of God." In one year, thirty thousand immigrants were served in some manner by the Bethel Ship and its staff.

In addition to a personal ministry to meet the needs of arriving immigrants and sailors on temporary visit, the Bethel Ship had other consequences, both religious and sociological. It is known that a number of early Swedish immigrants prior to the advent of the Bethel Ship had been influenced by and became members of the Methodist church in various parts of the country. This process would certainly have continued. Nevertheless, historians generally agree that the Bethel Ship was a major factor in the establishment of the Methodist Episcopal Church among Swedish immigrants wherever they colonized in sufficient numbers to make Swedish institutions possible. Through an aggressive program and dynamic leadership, the Bethel Ship became a channel for the missionary outreach of denominational Methodism. It contributed substantially to the development of Norwegian and Danish Methodism in America. Through a process of remigration, the Methodist Episcopal Church was introduced and established in the Scandinavian countries with the assistance of Swedish Methodist leadership for supervision and organization sent from America. By the counseling of arriving immigrants, and by the establishing of a network of ministers associated with the work of the Bethel Ship, principally Olof Hedstrom's brother Jonas, geographical patterns of settlement were organized in the Midwest. But we must first turn to the story of Peter Bergner and the humble beginnings of a movement with wide consequences and ramifications.

On a summer day, August 27, 1832, a square-rigged, multimasted vessel designated as a "Swedish barque" sailed into New York Harbor. It bore the name *Minerva*, and its port of embarkation had been Gothenburg, Sweden. In its crew was a mate (*styrman*) named Peter Bergner. The *Minerva* was obviously a cargo ship, but as was so often the case in those days, it also carried a limited number of passengers. Four of the six passengers are recorded in official arrival lists under the surname Berner, namely: Margareta Berner, 37; Anna H. Berner, 17; Johan Alfred Berner, 12; and Olivia Berner, 5.[3] There is ample justification for the assumption that they were Peter Bergner's family. The mangling of family names among arriving immigrants was a notoriously common experience, some carrying the variant through the remainder of their American sojourn, passing it on to their children. The name was often written as heard by the ear of the recording official or clerk—an ear untuned to foreign names, pronunciations, and accents. In this instance, the soft *g* of the Swedish Bergner was missed. Several years later, in 1850, a census taker recorded the name as Peter Berker. In the name as pronounced in America, the hard *g* was interpreted as *k* while the *n* was missed.

A more compelling reason for the assumption is the statement by J. T. Gracey in *Missions and Missionary Society of the Methodist Episcopal Church*, which reads: "August 26, 1832, he [Bergner] arrived with his family in New York City."[4] Further, sometime after the establishment of the Bethel Ship in 1845, Johan Alfred Bergner, then grown to young manhood, became the first class leader in the Bethel Ship Swedish congregation, an important spiritual office, as previously noted, in traditional Wesleyan Methodism. Later in life he traveled to San Francisco, where he founded a Swedish Methodist church in that community.[5]

We know little of Bergner's life before his coming to America. He was born in Gothenburg, Sweden, on July 29, 1797.[6] On February 5, 1826, Bergner was married to Margareta Andersdotter, with whom he had two children, Oliva and John Alfred. Margareta had a daughter, Anna H., from a previous marriage. Bergner was regarded as well educated by his American associates. Two chroniclers confirm this impression. The 1845 *Annual Report of the New York City Tract Society* says of him, "A Swede, after receiving a good education, became a wanderer in the world. At one time he was a soldier, at another a sailor." Gracey, a historian of the Missionary Society of the Methodist Episcopal Church, provides some of the most specific details available concerning the life of Bergner: "He had been a student in the University of Uppsala, where he was preparing for the ministry, though he did not take orders. He had an acquaintance with Hebrew, Greek, Turkish, Italian, Spanish, and English, and was known as 'Polyglot Peter.'"[7] One may surmise that the modern languages were acquired in Bergner's years of global travel. Language skills and his seafaring experiences served him well when he later became a port missionary.

Having tired of the sea and seeking a more normal family life, Peter Bergner resigned his post on the *Minerva* shortly after reaching America and established his home in New York. Though not mentioned elsewhere, there is no reason to doubt Newman's description of it as a boardinghouse, which provided needed income.[8] However, it was quite natural that Bergner should find some occupation related to the sea and ships. He became a marine carpenter, for which there must have been considerable demand, with the number of sailing vessels coming into the harbor constantly increasing. The remaining thirty-four years of his life were spent on the New York waterfront, where he became a familiar figure.

Life on the harbor was not without occupational hazards. Polyglot Pete was a gregarious individual, and drinking companions were readily available among sailors and dock workers. Though the accounts vary, it is generally agreed that alcohol was largely responsible for a series of three accidents that were destined to redirect the course of Bergner's life.

While repairing a ship, Bergner fell from the side of the hull to his float, on which his adze (a carpenter's tool for chipping) was laying edge-up. His knee struck the tool, fracturing the bone. Scarcely recovered and able to get about, he fell again and refractured the leg. After a second recovery, he had a further misfortune. While walking the deck of a moored vessel unloading a cargo of cotton one day, he was struck by a swinging bale. Again the knee was fractured in the same place. Bergner dispiritedly entered the hospital but was later discharged a transformed man who had found both physical and spiritual healing.[9]

Captain Roland Gelston was the human instrument of Bergner's life-transforming experience. In New York, the revivals of Charles G. Finney were still vivid memories.[10] Their pervasive spirit and influence were perpetuated in the churches of the city, generally through the New York City Tract Society (now the New York City Mission Society), an interdenominational agency that had been responsible for the invitation extended to Finney to work in New York. With this society, which included in its membership leaders in the political, financial, civic, and church life of the city, Charles Finney had developed a strong affinity. Volunteer and employed missionaries were trained in the art of tract distribution to convert the unchurched. There were not many churches in the city that did not have a committee of two or three persons related to the tract society and responsible for its work in the local church community. The society also provided for institutions and communities where no church existed. In 1844, Roland Gelston was listed in the records of the tract society as a representative of the Mariners' Methodist Episcopal Church.[11]

One day, while making his customary rounds of hospital wards, Gelston found Peter Bergner sleeping soundly.[12] He quietly laid a tract titled *The Conversation of an Infidel* on Bergner's chest and went away. When he awakened, Bergner found the tract, read it, and discovered it spoke to intellectual doubts with which he had been struggling. The next meeting between Bergner and Gelston seems nowhere to be recorded. However, a relationship was established, with profound consequences for Bergner's life. It also determined his future ties to the Methodist Episcopal Church.

With the zeal of a new convert, Peter Bergner became suddenly aware of the spiritual, moral, and social needs of a growing number of Swedish sailors coming into New York Harbor. In part, their increasing numbers were due to the shipping of iron ore from Sweden. In addition, though only a trickle prior to 1840, Swedish immigration was beginning to accelerate.[13] There was still no place in New York, or in America, where newly arrived Swedes could worship in their native language.

Impelled by his concern for their welfare, Peter Bergner held the first Swedish religious service in New York, evidently in 1844. It is quite possible that it was also the first Swedish-language service in America since those conducted in churches established by Sweden in the period of its colonization in Delaware and surrounding territory. Those churches had been conveyed to the Episcopal Church following the Revolutionary War. Bergner's service was held aboard a German vessel.[14] Five persons were present—four Swedish sailors and Peter Bergner. The service was simple, consisting of the singing of a few hymns, Bible reading, prayer, and the reading of one of Luther's sermons from the *Postilla*. At succeeding services, the attendance increased beyond Bergner's expectations. These early gatherings were held in unrecorded and random locations.[15]

"Afterwards," it is reported, "he obtained the use of a Floating Bethel on Sabbath mornings, and sometimes added exhortation to other exercises."[16] This statement, extracted from the 1845 *Annual Report of the New York City Tract Society*, provides important information on the origin of the Bethel Ship *John Wesley* and how it came into the possession of the Methodist Episcopal Church. The use of floating chapels for ministry to seamen was common; they were to be found in several American ports. There were at least two in New York Harbor. The Protestant Episcopal Church had a floating Church of Our Saviour moored at the foot of Pike Street in the East River. The Wesleyan Methodist Church had a floating chapel moored at the foot of Rector Street at Pier 11 on the

Peter Bergner

George Scott

The first Bethel Ship *John Wesley*, 1845. Courtesy
Swedish-American Historical Society.

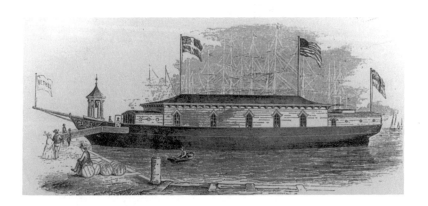

The second Bethel Ship *John Wesley*, 1857. Courtesy
Swedish-American Historical Society.

Castle Garden. Originally built as a concert hall, Castle Garden was the site of Jenny Lind's New York performances. In 1855, Castle Garden was converted to a registration center for immigrants and served in that capacity until 1892, when Ellis Island replaced it. Courtesy Collection of Advertising History, Archives Center, National Museum of American History, Smithsonian Institution.

Jenny Lind, ca. 1854. Courtesy H. C. Andersen Hus, Odense.

Jonas Hedstrom

Olof Gustaf Hedstrom, *bottom row, center*, and a consultation of
Swedish Methodist pastors in Chicago, 1865, to discuss the founding of a Swedish Methodist theological seminary. Courtesy Drew
University Library, Henry C. Whyman Swedish Methodist Collection, Madison, New Jersey.

North River (now Hudson River). Which floating bethel was
Bergner permitted to use? Since it was the latter bethel that
was later purchased by a missionary agency of the Methodist
Episcopal Church, it is a certainty that Peter Bergner had
secured its use for his Sunday morning Swedish services.
With this premise in mind, we now recall its origin.

The story of the conversion of an old hull bearing the name
Henry Leeds, about to be knocked to pieces, into a floating
chapel is told in an article published in 1844 in the December
issue of *Sailor's Magazine*, a New York monthly concerned
with the spiritual welfare of seamen.[17] Walking along the
wharves on the North River, a concerned member of the
Wesleyan Methodist Church saw the condemned brig and
wondered whether it might not be converted into a floating
bethel church for seamen. He shared his thought with several
fellow members of his denomination, which was an offshoot
of the Methodist Episcopal Church, with strong leanings
toward the "holiness" movement and policy differences with
the parent body. The result was the organization of the New
York Wesleyan Bethel Association, the purpose of which was
"to provide seamen with religious instruction in accordance
with the usages of the Wesleyan Methodist Church of the
United States of America; and to advance among them the
Temperance reformation." The unsigned article further states:
"The Association purchased the 'Henry Leeds' and fitted it
up after the English fashion, with plain and commodious
seats sufficient to accommodate five or six hundred persons.
It was opened for divine worship by a sermon and other
appropriate exercises on Thursday, the 21st ult. [November
21, 1844], and called by the name of the celebrated founder
of Methodism—'John Wesley.'"[18]

The cost of purchase and renovation was approximately
two thousand dollars. Readers were encouraged to make
contributions to defray expenses and were invited to visit the
John Wesley.

It would have been natural for Peter Bergner to have sought
space for his service in the newly renovated chapel. A Swed-

ish-language service would hardly compete with the program of the Wesleyan Bethel Association. Obviously, however, the association found some problems in developing its program, whereas Bergner could bring to the floating bethel a growing congregation. He had the further advantage of a natural constituency, inasmuch as his was the only regular Swedish-language service in America. It is not surprising, therefore, that approximately six months after inaugurating services, the New York Wesleyan Bethel Association was willing to sell the former *Henry Leeds*, now the Bethel Ship *John Wesley*, to the Asbury Society of the Methodist Episcopal Church.[19]

The Asbury Society had been organized about 1842 by representatives of Methodist Episcopal churches in New York City, clergy and lay, "for the purpose of increasing the number of churches where they were most needed."[20] Unlike the Missionary Society, which was a general agency serving the entire denomination, the Asbury Society was a local New York church extension organization. The availability of the Bethel Ship, for which the society paid twenty-five hundred dollars, was fortuitous.

Sometime in 1844 or early 1845, Peter Bergner saw that his intensely personal missionary project to seamen and immigrants had developed beyond his power to care for it. The prospects obviously warranted full-time professional leadership. He longed "to hear the Gospel preached there by some minister from his native land."[21] We must assume his decision to go to the Mulbery Street office of the Missionary Society of the Methodist Episcopal Church for advice and assistance was influenced by his friend and mentor, Captain Roland Gelston. Here he was met by Dr. David Terry, who was immediately responsive and encouraging.

Whether by providence or by coincidence, there was a man of Swedish birth serving in the ministry of the Methodist Episcopal Church in its New York Conference. Bergner was instructed to write to the Reverend Olof Gustaf Hedstrom in Prattsville, New York, where he was serving as pastor, with the assurance that Dr. Terry would also correspond with him.

Hedstrom's reactions were not encouraging. For ten years he had served churches in the Catskill Mountains of New York State with considerable success and personal satisfaction. He feared that he had lost the ability to preach properly in the Swedish tongue, since he could hardly recite the Lord's Prayer in that language. To him, the prospects were as "dark as a pocket."

The New York Annual Conference met in the Forsythe Street Methodist Episcopal Church in New York City on May 14, 1845. Dr. Terry was standing at the door, waiting for Hedstrom to arrive. No matter how reluctant Hedstrom was—for his prime desire was to return to his rural parish—he could hardly refuse Dr. Terry's invitation to accompany him to Peter Bergner's home, not far from the Bethel Ship. After introductions, Bergner and Hedstrom exchanged a few words in Swedish. Serious discussion concerning the mission to Scandinavian immigrants and seamen followed. Finally, the three knelt in prayer, which became a moving and deeply emotional experience. When they arose, all of Hedstrom's doubts and reservations had dissolved. He capitulated with the words, "I believe this to be of God. If the Bishop appoints me, I shall go to the Ship." When the appointments were read at the conclusion of the conference session, there was a new listing and a new assignment reading, Olof Gustaf Hedstrom— North River Mission.[22]

Sunday, May 25, 1845, was a notable day for Peter Bergner. It was the day the Reverend Olof G. Hedstrom conducted his first service on the Bethel Ship. Standing on the dock distributing tracts and inviting passing sailors to enter the ship was Dr. David Terry, who had developed a close identification with the project. Bergner was also aboard. It would be difficult to imagine him uninvolved as both the congregation (with no formal denominational affiliation as yet) and the Bethel Ship *John Wesley* were the fruit of Bergner's planning and labors. Hedstrom describes the gathering: "I found in the morning a congregation of seamen and landsmen, consisting chiefly of Swedes, but with them were also a few Danes and Norwegians."[23]

The development of the full Sunday program included a three o'clock service attended by persons from almost every European nation, a five o'clock service in German, and a well-attended English service in the evening. Social services and counseling supplemented the program of evangelism. The Bethel Ship became a hospitable haven for travel-weary, apprehensive immigrants.[24] The rest of the Bethel Ship story must be recounted largely in the context of Hedstrom's life and service. However, as we shall see, Peter Bergner continued to be a part of that story.

Methodism's new ministry of the New York Annual Conference, called the North River Mission, needed to take the next step. After May 25, it was imperative that the work be structured, and even institutionalized, to provide stability. A notice calling for a meeting on board the Bethel Ship on July 7, 1845, from noon to one, for the purpose of incorporation and the election of trustees, was posted on a prominent bulkhead of the ship by Hedstrom. Present in addition to Hedstrom and Bergner were Dr. David Terry, Jr., of the Missionary Society, Peter Dahlberg, and George B. Pollock, the latter associated with the Asbury Society. Hedstrom was appointed chairman, Pollock became the secretary, and Bergner and Dahlberg were designated to certify the actions of the meeting for legal and corporate purposes. Two actions were taken: (1) It was resolved that the society should be named The First North River Bethel Society of the Methodist Episcopal Church. (2) Nine influential New York Methodists were elected trustees, including David Terry and Roland Gelston, to whom Bergner was unforgettably indebted.

On July 11, 1845, corporate status was granted and the certificate signed proudly by Peter Bergner and Peter Dahlberg, with the signatures properly attested.[25]

In 1849, Peter Bergner, at the age of fifty-two, laid aside the tools of a marine carpenter to devote himself full time to the cause of Christ, working from the Bethel Ship. He accepted an appointment as missionary for the New York City Tract Society; the designation read: "Responsible for Swed-

ish and Immigrant work and the Bethel Ship *John Wesley*."[26]
As indicated earlier, the Tract Society had a committee in
each church to promote and supervise the work of that
society. Tract Society records state that the Bethel Ship committee consisted of Olof G. Hedstrom and John Harris, a
Norwegian serving as the first Sunday school superintendent
aboard the Bethel Ship. Bergner then officially became Hedstrom's first assistant.

It is interesting to note that in 1845 the Tract Society
reported distributing 320 tracts in the Swedish language.
Twenty years later, the year before Bergner died, the society
reported distribution of 14,078 tracts in Swedish. When
vessels from foreign shores, particularly Scandinavia, arrived
in the harbor, a rowboat alongside the Bethel Ship was
routinely prepared for its mission. It would be well stocked
with tracts in appropriate languages, as well as Bibles provided by the Marine and New York Bible Societies. Hedstrom,
or one of his assistants, with Bergner always as oarsman,
would board the vessel, secure permission from the captain
to speak to the crew and passengers, and with the tract offer
an invitation to visit the Bethel Ship.

On his sixty-ninth birthday, July 29, 1866, Peter Bergner
died. Having spent the last thirty-four years of his life in
America on the New York waterfront, it was appropriate that
the memorial service for this sailor, marine carpenter, and
port missionary should be held on the Bethel Ship. The
Reverend Hedstrom conducted the service and offered a
"powerful funeral sermon."[27]

The Annual Report of the New York City Tract Society for 1866
carried the following comment: "There were during the year
35 missionaries and 15 female assistants on the role [*sic*] of the
Society. One, the missionary to Swedish immigrants, after a
long illness, was removed by death in the 69th year of his age,
having been in the work of the Mission 17 years."[28]

6

The Bethel Ship John Wesley

As we have seen, floating chapels were established in several major ports during the nineteenth century. The designation "bethel" was common to both facilities and programs dedicated to Christian service and evangelism for visiting and resident seafarers. Bethel ships were an ingenious use for discarded vessels. Moored at piers, their visibility and easy access made such use particularly appropriate. We are fortunate in having both pictorial and verbal descriptions of the first Bethel Ship *John Wesley* and its successor of the same name a few years later.

Sven B. Newman, Hedstrom's first regularly appointed ministerial assistant in 1851, helps us visualize the interior of the converted brig named the Bethel Ship *John Wesley*.

The remarkable ship, originally named *Henry Leeds*, was converted to a church especially for seamen, and its name changed. With the exception of a mast at the bow, others had been removed. The cargo space below the deck had been renovated to serve as a sanctuary completely furnished with pulpit and pews. A room in the bow served as an office. On quarter-deck a cabin had been converted to a class room and a sexton's apartment. On the exterior, the bow was embellished with a carved human figure under the bowsprit. On both port and starboard sides of the bow, identical signs were inscribed— *Bethel Ship John Wesley* and an invitation to worship. American, Norwegian, Danish, and Swedish flags fluttered in the breezes. High on the remaining mast a blue and white *Bethel* flag was flown. Light was provided by skylights on the deck. The whole atmosphere was both attractive and inviting. A ramp which rose and fell with the tides, led from the dock to a door on the port side near the bow, providing an entrance to the sanctuary and office. Large iron chains secured the ship to the dock.[1]

The recycled ship was more fragile than it appeared. In a short time it began to leak and show signs of irreparable deterioration. In the early 1850s, Peter Bergner was heard to lament, "Why are the dwelling places of Jesus so poor?"[2] The Bethel Ship had to be placed in dry dock for caulking and repairs. These efforts proved temporary. In spite of its condition, the first Bethel Ship rendered exceptional service for eleven years to the ever-increasing number of Swedish immigrants and seamen visiting New York Harbor. Finally, a decision had to be made.

On June 17, 1856, the trustees of the First North River Bethel Society gathered aboard the ship. They spent some time evaluating "the extraordinary service of Pastor Hedstrom [on the] old craft" and took note of the undeniable reformation in the general habits and conduct among large numbers of seagoing men. They reviewed the Scandinavian work and "the fact that all Methodist missionaries to the Scandinavians at home and abroad have been set in motion by the labors of our missionary at the old ship." The conclusion was incontrovertible. A new ship had to be secured. The trustees pledged eighteen hundred dollars toward a total estimated cost of ten thousand dollars before concluding their meeting. Since both the New York and New York East conferences were about to meet, the trustees addressed the following resolution to them:

> That we recommend the subject of a new Bethel Ship to the hearty cooperation of our people, and that we pledge ourselves to assist in taking subscriptions and collections for this purpose. Send to—Bethel Ship, Carlton and Porter, 200 Mulberry Street, N.Y.[3]

The new Bethel Ship *John Wesley* was dedicated Tuesday afternoon, May 12, 1857.[4] The sermon was preached by the

Reverend Bishop Matthew Simpson, who sailed the next day
for Europe to visit mission fields, particularly in Germany,
Sweden, and Norway. The second Bethel Ship was far more
spacious and impressive, while retaining in general the func-
tional arrangement and appointments of the first. The sanctuary above the deck was given an ecclesiastical treatment, by
which its character and use were easily identified. "The
Swedish Bethel Ship" was the title of an article in which
Sailor's Magazine described the ship.

> As a ship it has a hull, but neither mast or rigging; as a church
> it has pews and pulpit, a conference room, and apartment for
> the sexton, but no steeple nor gallery. . . . The vessel lies with
> her bow to the wharf, from which you enter by a railed
> gangway. Two doors in the small building in front admit you
> by entry ways into the main room. Between the entries is the
> Pastor's study, on either side are lockers or cases for books and
> for the Sunday School library. The main room built upon the
> deck, is neatly done off with pews capable of accommodating
> some three hundred hearers; the pulpit being in the aft or
> stern end. Underneath this, and equally spacious, is the
> lecture room. The sexton's rooms are in the rear. On the bow is
> erected a belfry. On the bowsprit the Bethel flag invites the
> passerby to worship. The flags of Sweden and America float
> above the main building, as if to show two Christian nations
> uniting to protect their sailors in the worship of their common
> Lord.[5]

David Terry, the pastor to whom Bergner was referred
when he went to the Missionary Society of the Methodist
Episcopal Church for assistance, was a creative and influential city strategist for the Methodists in New York. He must be
given major credit for the development of the Bethel Ship
program. Wade Crawford Barclay, a historian of Methodist
missions, confirms Terry's role: "By his initiative the Bethel
Ship was purchased as a center for the seamen's mission."[6]
Terry was a staff member of the Missionary Society designated as "city missionary," and assigned to New York. He had

arrived at this position as a consequence of a fortuitous twist in his ministerial career. In 1831 he became a ministerial member of the New York Conference and was, as was Hedstrom four years later, appointed to serve a circuit in the Catskill Mountains. A financial stringency of undescribed nature compelled Terry to accept a more remunerative job in 1835 with a well-supported Protestant organization in New York City known as Refuge House that ministered to juvenile delinquents and vagrant children. Among other duties, Terry worked with rural pastors and churches to place city waifs in benevolent Christian homes. Terry would undoubtedly cultivate parishes known to him in the Catskills, several of which were or had been served by Olof Hedstrom, who would certainly have responded sympathetically and cooperatively. Further, Terry's exposure to moral and spiritual deprivation in the city was to determine the direction of his future ministerial career. Sometime before 1845, when released from earlier financial pressures, Terry accepted the post of city missionary at less than one-half his current salary.[7]

It was natural that Terry's mind should immediately leap to the Swede in the Catskill Mountains when confronted by Bergner's request. He could easily have verified that Hedstrom was the only fully ordained Methodist minister of Swedish birth in America—probably of any denomination. With confidence and determination, Terry began making plans even before he had a commitment from Hedstrom. Should Hedstrom be brought to New York, he would need some base of operation—a meeting facility more adequate than rental space for a Sunday service. What could be more appropriate than the Bethel Ship where Bergner's congregation was currently meeting? Further, it "was in the right place" to meet other needs that had been weighing heavily on his mind. Terry's negotiations with the Wesleyan Methodist Bethel Society are not recorded. Their tenure on the Bethel Ship had been barely six months. It had not been an unqualified success. The Wesleyans agreed to a sale, which was quickly consummated through the Asbury Society. The membership of that society was composed of several highly motivated Christian men, some quite affluent and influential, who had entered a supporting partnership with David Terry.[8]

Sometime during the several days of the 1845 New York Conference Annual Session, Terry met with the conference's Committee on Missions. Also present were members of the Asbury Society and Olof Gustaf Hedstrom. After the plan had been delineated, there was discussion and review. Hedstrom shared with the Committee on Missions his apprehension as he contemplated pastoral leadership of the Swedish congregation. He indicated the way in which he would approach this concern:

> As I had advised the Conference Missionary Committee that I had not used my native tongue or language for about twenty years, and should not attempt to preach in it, and especially because my conversation and godly edification to the time of my appointment had come wholly through the English language; but knowing a pious layman, I desired him to read a sermon to the congregation in their own tongue, to which I would add an exhortation and prayers in the same tongue.[9]

Parenthetically it should be noted that within three weeks, Hedstrom was preaching extemporaneously in Swedish, though never as fluently as in English. The conference committee gave its approval to the project to be known as The North River Mission, followed by final New York Conference approval and the appointment of Olof G. Hedstrom to the newly formed mission.

The North River Mission as originally designed by Terry and presented to the Committee on Missions was an inclusive program. In addition to the Swedish mission and a ministry to seafaring men generally, he envisioned service to a depressed and polyglot immigrant community along the shore of the North River in proximity of the Bethel Ship. Hedstrom describes that aspect of the plan:

> Among the causes which led to the establishment of this mission, a principal one was the destitute condition of the

foreign population on the North River side of this city. Here, the [*sic*] most of the merchantmen from France, Spain, Portugal, Italy, Prussia, Russia, Hamburg, Bremen, Denmark, Norway and Sweden, make their entrance; and here many of the families of foreigners reside. The spiritual necessities of these people had for some time been seen and deplored by some Christian philanthropists in this city, and a strong desire felt that something might be done for their benefit.[10]

In response to the general mandate, and in addition to the Swedish morning service, concerning which we shall explore in greater detail, three major programs were inaugurated with the immigrant community in mind. Children of immigrant families living in deprivation were an obvious concern. Even before Hedstrom's appointment, preliminary plans for the organization of a Sunday school had been set in motion. The minutes of the May 1845 meeting of the New York City Sunday School Society of the Methodist Episcopal Church reported a request — "Brother Williams applied for a grant of Sunday School books for use of a new school about to be opened on board the floating chapel."[11] This must have been approximately the time of the Bethel Ship acquisition.

Sunday school in the early and middle nineteenth century was drastically different from its later development in the religious education movement. It was primarily intended as a substitute for children who did not attend regular weekday schools.[12] Sunday schools shared the nature of "charity schools" established in poor neighborhoods and most often met apart from church buildings. The curriculum included alphabet primers, spelling books, and most importantly, pious tracts, stories, Bibles, and hymns for children. The teaching materials were inexpensively published by the Methodists' own Sunday School Union and tract societies, as well as the American Sunday School Union. Of this latter organization it was said, "It gives a child a testament and teaches him to read for 37 cents."[13] Because of prior preparation, including teacher recruitment, Hedstrom could report that a Sunday school opened on his second Sunday on the Bethel Ship. Its missionary character was particularly noted in a report: "The teachers take their dinners, and suppers too, with them and begin in the morning by calling at the homes for the children, and thus leading them to the school. They in many instances return them to their homes in like manner, to prevent them as far as may be from running in the highway of sin, at least on the Lord's day."[14]

In the course of pastoral visitation, Hedstrom entered a basement apartment and found it to be the residence of ten parents and twenty-four children. Twelve to fifteen were recruited that day for the Sunday school.

A Sunday afternoon service replicated Pentecost when persons with different native languages, under the influence of shared spirit, could worship together. It was a service to which crew members of foreign visiting vessels were especially invited. Hedstrom describes the service:

> At three o'clock our service commences, and at this might be found at times persons from almost every European nation. Great Britain, Germany, France, Switzerland, Holland, Norway, Sweden, Denmark, Finland, Prussia, and Italy; and although all of these could not perfectly understand English, yet by the means of the Bible and Tract societies, we were enabled to present to all, portions of the glad tidings, by which they might come to the possession of the great salvation.[15]

The linguistic skills of Peter Bergner must have been amply utilized for the benefit of many. Others with some limited knowledge of English also assisted their countrymen. Somehow, with ingenuity and imagination, the challenge was met. The polyglot nature of the Bethel Ship program continued in the early years. As late as 1849, Hedstrom was "cheered to hear the mingled voices from several nations singing and proclaiming the Gospel, each in a native tongue."[16]

The German segment of the immigrant community was probably the largest, and also the most responsive, of the non-Scandinavian groups. Two German Methodist congregations had been inaugurated in New York in 1841 and 1843, respectively—primarily through the influence of German immigrants in Ohio, where Methodism had taken root among Germans beginning in 1835. William Nast was appointed missionary to Germans by the Ohio Conference on August 19, 1835.

Neither of the New York congregations was so located that it might serve the Bethel Ship community. The two German pastors, John Christian Lyon and F. C. Hartmann, were prevailed upon to share the responsibility for a German Sunday service aboard the Bethel Ship at five o'clock—later advanced to two o'clock. Within three months, two hundred Germans gathered on the Bethel Ship every Sunday.[17] The resident German population in New York numbered sixty thousand. In addition, during 1846, one hundred vessels entered New York Harbor with crews who understood only German. In 1847 it was reported that a dozen persons were received into a German Methodist society in western Ohio, "all of whom professed to have been awakened in our Bethel Ship . . . soon after their arrival from Germany."[18] That year, the Bethel Ship trustees made a financial provision for the employment of a German colporteur to work on the ship. On Friday, April 6, 1849, a "'North River German Mission' was opened under most favorable auspices." The German congregation developed on the Bethel Ship was transferred, along with its class meeting and prayer meeting, to an acquired facility called The Upper Room, at 160 Washington Street.[19]

Temperance was an important part of the Bethel Ship ministry. Seamen in port with time and some money on their hands were notorious alcohol abusers. Monday evening was dedicated to the cause with a temperance lecture followed by pledge signing. The pledge may well have been the one distributed by the Marine Temperance Society of the port of New York, which in 1845 reported seventeen thousand registered signers. "Believing the use of intoxicating drinks to be not only unnecessary, but injurious to the social and religious interests of man: I do hereby agree, looking to God for help, that I will not use them myself, nor provide them as an article of entertainment for my friends, and that I will make special efforts to promote habits of temperance among seamen."[20] Within a year, Hedstrom could report four hundred signed pledges aboard the Bethel Ship.

Hedstrom regarded the Monday meetings as part of his evangelical program, as indicated by his 1848 report to the Missionary Society. "Our temperance meetings are conducted on strictly religious principles, and instances have occurred when signing the pledge has been succeeded by a crowd rushing to our altar for prayers."[21] Prayer meetings and class meetings completed the weeknight schedule. There seemed always to be a service to which passengers and crews could be invited when Hedstrom and Bergner boarded the arriving vessels.

The Bethel Ship was barely in place when Swedish emigration became numerically significant. Nils William Olsson suggests that on the basis of New York ship manifests, approximately four thousand Swedes arrived in that port between 1820 and 1850. In the five years before the establishment of the Bethel Ship, recorded Swedish arrivals averaged 67 annually, with 93 in 1845. A dramatic increase to 902 in 1846 was due largely to the exodus from Sweden of members of the Eric Jansson sect.[22] In addition, Hedstrom was developing a fruitful and important ministry to Scandinavian seamen. Speaking to a Seamen's Chaplains Convention in 1846, he estimated that twelve hundred Scandinavian seamen came to New York annually. Of the one hundred ships (seventy Swedish, twenty Norwegian, and ten Danish), each carried a crew of about twelve.[23]

It was the existence of a Swedish congregation that had given rise to the North River Mission. In the end, the major focus of that mission was to minister to Swedish seamen and their families, and especially to immigrants from Sweden. Continuing his historical account just one year after its inception, Hedstrom offered an interesting if somewhat biased rationale in defense of the Swedish program:

Especially did they deem it important that some place might be established where the worship of God should be conducted in the Swedish language. With these impressions, it was resolved that an effort should be made to provide the means of salvation for Swedish seamen, as well as Swedish residents. This was as it should be; for perhaps there is no nation to whom the Protestant world is under more solemn and weighty obligation than to Sweden. The noble and successful resistance they made to Popish tyranny, under their king, the immortal Gustavus Adolphus, who was at the head of the Protestant League, in the thirty-year's war, should never be forgotten. The peace of Westphalia, in 1648, which was dictated by Swedish ambassadors, established a new league of nations in Europe, and gave to all Christian Churches in Germany political and civil equality.[24]

The Swedish ministry provided stability and permanence to the Bethel Ship program. There were several bethel missions serving seafaring persons at the port of New York and elsewhere. None had the long tenure or the enduring consequences associated with the Bethel Ship *John Wesley*. The broad spectrum of ethnic ministries with which it began narrowed rapidly, and the Scandinavian work became its central focus. The relationship of the Swedish congregation to the North River Bethel Society was affirmed in the election of John Harris to its board. Norwegian by birth and married to a Swedish woman, he was an early member of the Swedish congregation. Harris was appointed the first Sunday school superintendent.[25] It is Hedstrom's Swedish ministry to which we now turn.

7

From North River to Swedish Bethel

Hedstrom's original appointment to the North River Mission was designed to meet a broad variety of needs in a multiethnic immigrant community. Four years later, the wording of the assignment was changed to Swedish Bethel. Given the initial Swedish congregation, escalating Swedish immigration, and a Swedish pastor of Hedstrom's caliber and energy, the direction of the Bethel Ship ministry was inevitable, if not predictable. It should be noted that from the beginning, the Swedish congregation was the only Bethel Ship membership officially recorded and reported.

Two parties arriving from Sweden in 1845 and receiving hospice on the Bethel Ship were forerunners of a burgeoning Swedish emigration movement that became known in that country as "America Fever." Each party played a notable role in Swedish immigrant history. Less than two months after the inauguration of the Bethel Ship program, on August 11, 1945, the bark *Superb* sailed into the harbor with Peter Cassel and twenty other Swedes, mainly relatives and neighbors. Most were from Kisa Parish in Östergötland, Sweden.[1] Influenced by letters from earlier emigrants Polycarpus von Schneidau and Gustaf Unonius, they intended to settle in Wisconsin. While recuperating on the Bethel Ship from the long voyage, Cassel and his compatriots met Peter Dahlberg, who had explored substantial portions of the Midwest and who was awaiting the arrival of his wife and family. Dahlberg's glowing account of the rich Iowa soil impressed Cassel, causing the party to change its travel plans. They established New Sweden in Jefferson County, Iowa, and became the "first emigrant group to leave a defined area in Sweden to settle in a specific locale in the U.S."[2] In the context of Swedish Methodism, we shall meet Cassel again.

Of even greater import to Swedish immigrant history was the arrival of Olof Olsson and his family aboard the brig *Neptune* on December 15, 1845.[3] Olsson described his initial introduction to America as "two hours of darkness." Unable to communicate, Olsson and his family did not know where to turn. A child of eight sensed their predicament. She took Olsson by the hand and led the family to the Bethel Ship and its "Swedish priest."[4] The family consisted of Olsson's wife, Anna Marie, a daughter, Beata, age nine, and a son, Jonas, age seven. They were given living quarters on the Bethel Ship in back of the sanctuary. Two weeks later, on December 31, Olsson wrote a letter to his mother and family in Sweden: "[Hedstrom] met me with such charity, both in counsel and deeds, that I have often been moved to tears, for we, like faithful Abraham, did not have a footboard to alight on in the strange land and, like Jesus, no place to lay our head."[5]

Olof Olsson was a follower and trusted lieutenant of Eric Jansson, the founder and leader of a radical pietistic *läsare* sect in Sweden. Jansson had placed considerable distance between the main body of *läsare* pietists and his movement. Olsson had been sent to America to explore a suitable location with available land upon which the Janssonists could establish a religious community. Bizarre behavior in Sweden, including book burning, had aroused hostility and persecution of the Janssonists by church and civil authorities. Continued practice of their faith in Sweden had become untenable.

The larger portion of Olsson's letter to Sweden contained a glowing description of Methodist worship and spiritual practices aboard the Bethel Ship. Olsson had engaged Hedstrom in religious conversation for "days and hours." He was under no illusions concerning the Janssonist reaction to his favorable comments about Hedstrom and his services on the Bethel Ship. "Friends, you may well wonder how it is with me, whether or not I have been overstrained by something, that I, as my words now bear witness, should have confidence in a Swedish priest. But take note that this man is . . . different from a Lutheran priest."[6] That Olsson's positive description of Methodist worship and preaching was circulated among Janssonists in Sweden is evident. Before leaving for America in April 1846, Jansson wrote a long letter to his followers and included a list of nine subjects about which they were to pray. The seventh prayer was "that those bewildered followers who have been led astray by the seductions of Pastor Hedstrom should be brought back to the fold."[7]

The Olssons remained guests on the Bethel Ship for several weeks. Inevitably, a warm and trusting friendship developed. In temporal matters, Hedstrom was helpful. Temporary employment was secured for both Olsson and a fellow traveler, Erik Adolph Hellsten. Free schooling for Beata and her brother was also provided. Hedstrom shared information from his brother, Jonas, about the fertile plains of the military tract in Illinois. As soon as the spring thaw made canal travel possible, Olsson left his family on the Bethel Ship and set out for the Midwest and a meeting with Jonas Hedstrom in Victoria, Illinois. The profound effect of the Hedstrom connection linking New York and Victoria was thus inaugurated, establishing a pattern of Swedish settlement that lasted for several decades.

In late spring of 1846, Eric Jansson arrived in New York with his family. Hedstrom invited him to share the Bethel Ship pulpit, but Jansson seemed to prefer to hold services in the homes of Swedish residents. During the period in which Jansson remained in New York, he is alleged to have had some success in winning adherents. Considerable numbers of Janssonists emigrated from Sweden in the summer and fall of 1846. They were joined by hundreds of others seeking brighter economic prospects for themselves and their families.

In 1850, the Methodist Missionary Society of the Methodist Church took an action designed to strengthen Swedish work aboard the Bethel Ship. Undoubtedly, the action also reflected concern for the physical welfare of the indefatigable missionary carrying an increasingly heavy burden. "At a meeting of the General Missionary Committee in May 1850, an appropriation was made, in view of increasing labors of brother Hedstrom, and the opening doors among his countrymen, for the support of an additional missionary."[8] There was, surprisingly, one other fully ordained Swedish Methodist minister in America. He was a member of the Alabama Conference in the Methodist Episcopal Church, South, which in 1846 had separated from the northern branch of Methodism on the issue of slavery. Within days of the action by the General Missionary Committee, the Reverend Sven Bernhard Newman (Nyman), serving the Landerdale Circuit over the border in Mississippi, received a letter from Olof G. Hedstrom. Newman had just observed a day of fasting and prayer in which he had experienced strong nostalgic feelings for Sweden.[9]

Before emigration at age thirty in 1842, Newman had been restless both vocationally and spiritually. He was a teacher and master in a school he established. Earlier, he had been a bookkeeper and clerk for a wholesaler and served a stint at the Russian Consulate in Stockholm. Encouraged by his previously emigrated brother, Karl Ludvig, who was a merchant in Mobile, Alabama, Sven closed his school and set out for America. Karl Ludvig and his American wife were ardent members of the Methodist Episcopal Church, in which he had become a class leader. Sven Newman soon became a member of the Methodist church and a participant in his brother's class. Accustomed to daily Bible reading and spiritual commentary in his school, public testimony in his Methodist class seemed natural. With increased language facility, Newman began cautiously to consider a ministerial career. Encouraged by pastoral leadership within the conference, Newman dissolved a grocery store partnership and began serious study in the required conference course. In 1845, having achieved a local preacher's license, he was received into the Alabama Conference on trial and sent to assist on a circuit in northern Florida.[10]

Newman had been discovered by a New Yorker in 1846. A representative of the Methodist Book Concern making an official visit to the Alabama Annual Conference, Mr. Tippet noticed Sven Newman and engaged him in conversation. Normally, a young first-year probationary member with a local preacher's license would not be very visible, but the Swede was easily recognized. Tippet spoke about the new Bethel Ship work and even suggested that Newman might be useful to the project. The comment was taken lightly.[11]

Hedstrom's letter was taken more seriously. Newman felt committed to his current appointment for the conference year. At the next session of the Alabama Annual Conference in January 1851, he was released with a complimentary resolution that read in part: "In view of the urgent call for his services among his own countrymen . . . we dare not refuse to allow him to respond to the call, which we consider as eminently providential and accordingly take leave of him with cordial affection and recommend him to the kind and fraternal regard of the Ministers and members of the M.E. Church North."[12] In short time, Newman was welcomed at 4 Carlisle Street, New York, by Olof and Caroline Hedstrom, their son, Wilbur, and adopted daughter, Maria Elisabeth.[13] They began their joint ministry by alternating preaching both in Swedish and English and in going out to meet arriving vessels carrying Scandinavian emigrants and seamen. Newman enjoyed a long and fruitful ministry in developing Swedish Methodism as a pastor, organizer, and builder of churches, district superintendent in the Midwest and finally as Chicago city missionary. He served two terms as Hedstrom's assistant on the Bethel Ship.

The nature of the Bethel Ship programs reflected adaptations to changed realities. The Sunday school is an excellent example. Originally designed to meet the needs of disadvantaged children, the Bethel Ship Sunday school of 1851 responded to a new challenge. The disadvantaged were now immigrants who neither spoke nor understood English. In his report to the Missionary Society, Hedstrom indicated the change: "We have a flourishing Sunday School, consisting mostly of Swedes and Norwegians of whom many are adults that learn the English language." Frederick Kron, a child of nine years, was brought to America by his parents in 1851. They immediately affiliated with the Bethel Ship, "probably because it was the only Swedish congregation in that place." Fred later described his Bethel Ship Sunday school experience:

> We were classified in accordance with our knowledge of the English language, though age was given some consideration. Nevertheless I was seated beside an older lady (*gammal gumma*) sixty to seventy years of age. We did not get along. I remember well that we did not speak a word to one another for several years. The school's superintendent was John Harris, a Norwegian by birth who was a God fearing and kind man. My teacher was Tom Smith, a native of Denmark, also God fearing and humble. This was my childhood relationship to the Bethel Ship.[14]

The textbook used was well suited to the teaching of both language and religion. The American Bible Society had produced a New Testament in both languages—Swedish and English—in parallel columns. Those books used in Sunday school were provided through a gift of six hundred dollars from Jenny Lind, "to be used in the purchase of Bibles for distribution to poor immigrants." According to Kron, the bilingual New Testament was the sole Sunday school text.[15]

Olof Hedstrom's concept of his mission is reflected in his multiform activities. First and foremost, he was concerned about the salvation of souls. His reports to his superiors and officers of the Missionary Society were about revivals and conversions. His theological thought had developed in the Charles G. Finney genre. The genteel and comfortable, charged with saving the souls of persons in every condition of life, discovered the horrible circumstances of immigrant masses. Carroll Smith Rosenberg roots a variety of New York City charitable and social service agencies organized in the mid-nineteenth century to the evangelical revival.[16] Many of these organizations are still in existence. When church people went to save souls in deprived areas of the city, they discovered poverty, physical suffering, and sordid conditions that compassionate Christians could not ignore. For Hedstrom, serving human need was part and parcel of the Gospel. More than one generation, without regard to denominational affiliation, held Olof Hedstrom in high honor and profound debt.

Peter Bergner completed a monthly report to the Missionary Society in 1851, when Hedstrom was absent because of a temporary illness. He rejoiced that so many sea captains were attending prayer meetings. It was a good sign, since sailors generally followed the captains. He reported with somewhat less enthusiasm certain aspects of his labors: "Some have come penniless and speechless. . . . For when they come, poor and miserable, almost everybody is willing to show them to the Bethel Ship, telling them that it is our duty to take care of them. I have thought sometimes the Ship has become a regular poor house."[17] Olof Hedstrom, more sanguine and possibly more compassionate, in a later report proclaimed, "The Bethel Ship is at once the hospital for the bodies and souls of the people for whom it was established. In the nature of the case it must be so."[18]

Most Swedish immigrants were speechless on arrival, but not all were penniless. They often came with modest resources secured from the sale of farmland and other property or with savings and borrowed money. These immigrants, too, were vulnerable. Rosenberg, a social historian, states, "By 1849 the number and needs of these new arrivals had become New York's single most discordant reality."[19] Part of that reality concerned predatory forces ready to victimize defenseless immigrants.

Swedes, and Scandinavians generally, were more fortunate than other nationals. Hedstrom, Bergner, and later Newman tried to meet every vessel carrying them into New York Harbor. After welcoming the new arrivals and providing some necessary information, the three invited immigrants to the Bethel Ship for worship and further assistance. Information about the helpful presence of Hedstrom in New York had been widely circulated in Sweden through newspaper reports and immigrant letters. One such letter advised that "in Gothenburg make contact for passage with Captain Erikson; he is reliable. In New York see Olof Hedstrom at the Bethel Ship. Beware of ship runners and land agents including those that speak Swedish. If you get lost, go down to the shore when ships are seen and call *Norsk Man* and soon someone will appear who speaks Swedish."[20]

In 1847, the New York State Assembly meeting in Albany publicly recognized the problem of immigrant exploitation and appointed a committee to investigate "frauds upon emigrant passengers arriving in this State." The committee reported notorious exploitation by the city's criminal and marginal business interests. The report led to action that eliminated the casual and haphazard debarkation of passenger arrivals along the waterfront piers. Castle Garden was designated as a central, safer, and more orderly point of immigrant entry.[21] Dr. Durbin, the Methodist missionary executive, had observed the immigrant tidal wave with compassionate concern: "The Strangers, who will remember them? Pastor Hedstrom, as usual, has been looking after the Scandinavians."[22]

The scope and variety of services rendered by the Bethel Ship are not easily described. Weary and often ill after the long and arduous ocean voyage, the newcomers needed physical care. Temporary and sometimes permanent housing had to be found. Unable to speak English, they were in need of an interpreter. Destitute, many required financial assistance. Fearful and lonely, they often needed a friendly counselor who spoke their language to provide assurance. Having no permanent address, the immigrants found that the Bethel Ship became their post office. Strangers in the land, they also needed travel guidance and assistance. Indeed, as others have suggested, the Bethel Ship provided the services of a Swedish Consulate.

Hedstrom was often stressed to the point of exhaustion, with consequent health problems: "The correspondence of this mission increases every year. The labors of the missionary in his study alone, where he must receive officers and crew, strangers from far and near, answer their enquiries, resolve their doubts, instruct their ignorance, and lead them to the Lamb of God, are sufficient to engross the time, and exhaust the strength of one man."[23]

The work was demanding, but also rewarding. Among the passengers who arrived aboard a vessel in 1853 was a twelve-year-old girl whose mother had died during the passage. The ship's captain took her to Hedstrom to provide care through some suitable employment. With the assistance of a ministerial colleague in upstate New York, the girl was placed in a comfortable Christian home. Ten years later, Hedstrom addressed a preacher's meeting in Buffalo. A young pastor insisted upon taking Hedstrom to his home, where there was someone eager to meet him. It was a joyous reunion. The twelve-year-old girl was now a cultivated and well-educated minister's wife.[24]

Hedstrom was an assiduous pastor. Though most Scandinavian immigrants were in transit to the West, the resident New York Scandinavian community continued to increase. For twenty years the Bethel Ship had the only Swedish worshiping congregation in the region, with Hedstrom as pastor and spiritual leader for the entire Scandinavian community. As such, he conducted marriages, baptisms, and funerals— especially funerals. We note an 1850 comment:

In no society that we know of, have we ever witnessed such numerous calls to aid in burying the dead as in this mission. May this paragraph lead some "Joseph of Aramathea" to give us a place of burial—a lot in Greenwood—to such of our sailors and stranger brethren as die among us, far from their kindred and native country. The case of sick strangers have imposed a mournfully pleasing task upon us; and most gladly do we here declare that the ready, cheerful, and gratuitous service of our American physicians are above all praise. We cannot but honour them exceedingly.[25]

Monthly reports of pastoral activities were made to the Missionary Society. Its house journal, the *Missionary Advocate*, included one such itemized report in 1851:

    Visited: 16 vessels
            43 Boarding Houses
            30 families of seamen
            21 families of Landsmen
            Once — Naval Hospital
            Twice — The Sailor's Retreat
            Once — Wards Island
            Five times — Williamsburgh, Brooklyn and Jersey City
            Distributed 600 Tracts
            3 copies of Scripture
            12 other books[26]

Indulgence and improvidence have traditionally characterized seamen in port. To combat sailors' reckless spending, leaders of New York's Bethel Union and the Port Society, both interdenominational, established an institution in 1829, still prominent in the New York financial community today, called the Seamen's Bank for Savings.[27] The Bethel Ship entered a program of collaboration with the Seamen's Bank with beneficial consequences. *The Missionary Advocate* in March 1855 carried the following in its Seamen's Department: "The Bethel Ship, N.Y., of which Rev. O. G. Hedstrom is pastor, continues to exert an increasing influence for good both upon sailors and landsmen. Some correct data are afforded to show the good effected in one point by the efforts chiefly of this mission from the fact, that since its commencement about one million dollars have been deposited in the Seamen's Saving Bank by Scandinavian sailors."[28]

Publishing in the Swedish language in nineteenth-century America was initiated by Hedstrom to increase the effectiveness of the Bethel Ship ministry. Since the invention of movable type, the printed word has always supplemented the spoken word. Distribution of tracts and Scripture portions was the period style. Through the assistance of the Missionary Society, the *Swedish-English New Testament* was published in 1851 by the American Bible Society. David Terry wrote a letter to the Tract Society of the Methodist Episcopal Church dated April 11, 1853, in which he supported the appeal of O. G. Hedstrom that they acquire "a forent [font] of type adapted to the work of printing in the German, Swedish and Danish languages." The letter further stated, "Now whilst he has a translator in his hands, and has a Swedish compositor within his reach, whom we could employ in our concern, and have control, if we move quickly."[29]

The translator was Jacob Bredberg, an Uppsala-educated pastor who had served for twenty years as a vicar in the Swedish church. He emigrated to America in 1853 and was quickly recognized for his eloquence and literary talents. Just as quickly he was at work with Hedstrom on the Bethel Ship translating tracts, John Wesley's sermons, and other writings, including his *Plain Account of Christian Perfection*, Charles Wesley's hymns, and "some of our best works on experimental religion."[30] Though not an enthusiastic Methodist, Bredberg, in addition to considerable translation, did serve brief pastorates in Jamestown, New York, and Chicago. Before becoming the rector of the Ansgarius Scandinavian Episcopal Church in Chicago, he edited the first Swedish Methodist hymnal, including translations of hymns in Methodist usage. In a letter to Eric Norelius almost a year after beginning, Bredberg commented, "I have recently completed a translation of Smith's 'Reasons for Becoming a Methodist'. . . . In addition I have translated several tracts (10 or 12) and sermons by Wesley, so that Hedstrom feels I am very industrious. . . . I am doing much work for the Methodist Church."[31]

Separate Norwegian services (probably class meetings) began on the Bethel Ship in 1856. A small group, including Thomas Smith, Hans Christian, and H. Larsen, made arrangements with the assistance of John Harris, a leader in the

Bethel Ship congregation from its earliest days.[32] This is of interest because post-Bethel Ship congregations were structured separately—Norwegian-Danish and Swedish. We should not infer that the action represented tensions in the Bethel Ship program. Rather, it was a reflection of political and cultural circumstances in their native lands. For four centuries, Norway had been a Danish dependency. Through the peace of Kiel during the Napoleonic wars, Norway was transferred to the Swedish crown following hostilities between Sweden and Denmark. Quite apart from that, while sharing common Scandinavian roots, each country in the natural course of development had acquired language and cultural distinctions. Norway finally achieved its independence in 1906.

The story of the extension of the Bethel Ship influence to the Midwest and across the ocean into Scandinavian countries will be told in later chapters. Olof Hedstrom was inevitably involved. Correspondence kept him informed of the distant missions. He became the nexus between the missions and the Missionary Society, which on Hedstrom's recommendation began modest funding. No one was better qualified to provide general oversight than Hedstrom. In the early 1850s, he was designated a superintendent of the Scandinavian mission by the society. Hedstrom was given considerable authority—even the power to override decisions made by regional Methodist church administrators when thought detrimental to the progress of the work.[33]

It was in this capacity that Hedstrom was sent on a series of missionary journeys in the early 1850s. In Boston and neighboring communities he organized two Methodist classes, though no church was immediately established, probably because continuing leadership was unavailable.[34]

Two visits to Jamestown, New York, and neighboring Chandler Valley, Pennsylvania, were especially fruitful. Swedes who had reached as far west as Buffalo began to settle in Jamestown. In 1850, the Swedish colony numbered 250; by 1875, the colony had grown to 22,000, almost half the population.

In June 1851, Hedstrom, the first Swedish pastor to go to Jamestown, held a service in a private home. A continuing class meeting was held in the basement of the local Methodist church. The following year, in early November 1852, he made a more extended visit in the course of which he formally founded a Swedish Methodist Church. Reporting to the Missionary Society, Hedstrom stated that he had preached twenty-seven sermons, celebrated the Sacrament of Holy Communion seven times in six places to 270 persons, baptized sixteen children, married three couples, and visited from house to house—and all within a two-week period. He arrived in Chicago before the middle of November. His report concluded with the comment that his health had improved.[35]

Olof Hedstrom remained in Chicago several days. An unanticipated opportunity to conduct services for the Swedish community met with an exceptionally good response. After traveling the Victoria Circuit of Swedish Methodist churches with Jonas, the two brothers went to Chicago, where Olof resumed earlier preaching services, this time in the Seaman's Bethel Chapel. Here he founded the Swedish Methodist Church of that city in December 1852. On Hedstrom's arrival home, Sven Newman was dispatched to Chicago to become its first pastor.[36]

In connection with Hedstrom's general supervision of an expanding Scandinavian Methodism, it is appropriate to call attention to his role in the recruitment and training of pastors. In one of its reports the Missionary Society proclaimed, "Another missionary has gone out from Hedstrom's Theological Seminary as he sometimes calls his ship when speaking of the number who have gone out to preach the word, who were first born, or rather born again in her."[37]

Hedstrom was an astute judge of character and talent. Biographical sketches of Swedish Methodist preachers in the Midwest and in Scandinavian countries record the conversion of many on the Bethel Ship and their spiritual and practical tutelage under Hedstrom. Several were employed by the Missionary Society for assistance on the Bethel Ship while serving an apprenticeship.[38]

The frequency and variety of religious services aboard the Bethel Ship must have amazed more arriving immigrants than Jonas Wallengren. He wrote his impressions to his father, a parish pastor in Sweden: "We have just had matins and the New Testament is sold here in both English and Swedish for *1 riksdaler 24 skilling* Swedish money. Swedish is on one page and English on the other page, and many tracts are given to emigrants in Swedish, English and German tongues. The Swedes have services here three times on Sundays and meetings during the week. Often they meet every evening."[39]

The Sunday morning service of common worship (*allmänna gudstjänsten*) was the heart of the Bethel Ship ministry from the beginning. There were elements with which the immigrant could identify. The hymnal was *Svenska psalmboken*, used by the Lutheran Church of Sweden. Familiar Bible passages were read from a large pulpit Bible, the gift of a Swedish sea captain. The order and language of Holy Communion came from the Swedish Lutheran liturgy.

But there were also differences. Reactions varied with the inclinations of the immigrant. Large numbers came with prior exposure to the virile pietism of contemporary Sweden. Others were staunch Lutherans. At the Bethel Ship they were confronted with a new element, revivalism, so much a part of American religious life for two hundred years. Hedstrom was a revivalist preacher who saw no conflict between experiential religion and Lutheranism. He acknowledged his indebtedness to Luther and insisted in discussion with an immigrant, "If I were a Lutheran, I would be a good one." However, he was also a Methodist partisan. Methodist custom included celebration of Holy Communion the first Sunday of every month. Though the language of the service was familiar, its Methodist interpretation was made explicit. In his first quarterly report, in 1845, Hedstrom commented: "My Swedish congregation has steadily increased, and has exceeded my expectations. I have administered the holy sacrament at three

different times to them: and beginning by holding a preparatory service with them in the morning at which I explained to
these children of the Reformation and members of the national Church, the sense we entertain of this sacred rite."[40]

The ministry of Hedstrom and the Bethel Ship was gratefully received by immigrants and applauded on both sides of
the Atlantic. Swedish immigration historians have given generous attention to Hedstrom's significant role. However, Hedstrom did have detractors among devotees of two other
denominational groups—Lutherans and Baptists. In general, the criticism was muted. It was difficult to press it vigor-
ously, partly because Hedstrom himself was by nature irenic
rather than polemic. Eric Norelius, a young immigrant with a
scholarly interest in religion, engaged Hedstrom in discussion three days after arrival. Norelius noted in his diary:
"After some further conversation with regard to doctrinal
matters, I found that we were not in agreement, but he was
friendly and courteous nevertheless."[41]

Norelius was himself to play an important role in immigrant history. One of the founders of the Augustana Synod of
the Lutheran church, he was twice its president and its prime
historian. He attended the Bethel Ship service on his first
Sunday in New York, November 3, 1850. It was Communion
Sunday. His evaluation, written forty years later, confirms his
diary notation, and it is of interest. "The order of the service
was not precisely the one common in Sweden—it was somewhat modified. His sermon was heart warming; but the
content confused, without proper differentiation between
law and Gospel; the thought process was unclear, and his
speech though broken Swedish was fairly well understood. In
private conversation, he impressed us as devoutly spiritual—
though not a fanatic."[42] Concerning the Bethel Ship and its
program, Norelius judged that "the design was remarkably
well conceived and the mission undoubtedly could have accomplished more if executed by more skillful instruments."[43]

In the light of his experience in the staid and sedate
Lutheran service, coupled with his scholarly mind, Norelius's

reaction is understandable. Hedstrom's revivalist sermon, often extemporaneous, troubled Norelius. Hedstrom was preaching for a verdict. He would insist that he preached both law and gospel, the law inducing a sense of sin and guilt of conscience leading to repentance, thus preparing the sinner to receive the gospel of forgiveness and redemption through the love of Christ.

When one considers the totality of Hedstrom's ministry, both temporal and spiritual, it is difficult to sustain the rather harsh implication of Norelius's evaluation. He did recognize Hedstrom's place in history when, in his major work, he included Holger Olson's biographical address at the dedication of a monument at Hedstrom's grave in Greenwood Cemetery, Brooklyn—though with the caveat, "It is naturally strictly Methodist, but likewise of interest to Lutheran readers because of his historic content."[44]

Another portrait of Olof Hedstrom deserves to be noted. We become acquainted with Frederick Kron when, as a child of nine, he was enrolled in the Bethel Ship Sunday school in 1850. When he came home from the Civil War in 1865, he was appointed class leader for the Bethel Ship Brooklyn contingent. As an adult he was a confidant and admirer of Hedstrom. In 1895, when Swedish Methodists celebrated the fiftieth anniversary of the Bethel Ship ministry, Kron had the longest record of continuous relationship to it. He was therefore requested to write a history and personal recollection for the Swedish-American periodical *Sändebudet*. His account is somewhat rambling but rich in insights about ancillary services such as the Methodist love feasts, the high regard in which Hedstrom was held by the American community, and several significant episodes. About Hedstrom's preaching he comments:

> He was not concerned whether or not he went beyond the boundaries of his text, if only he might reach the sinner's heart. At every service the Ship was filled to capacity. In those days the harbor swarmed with Swedish and Norwegian sail-

ing vessels. No one could interpret the seaman's emotions in a more masterful way. He reminded them of prayers and promises made at sea in the height of a wild and raging storm. . . . As a speaker he was without doubt extremely gifted. His sermons at Christmas, Easter, Good Friday, were excellent and instructive. He understood how to present his message in a simple, attractive and graphic fashion in which people felt personally involved.[45]

8

Jenny Lind

She was called "the Swedish Nightingale" and possessed a coloratura soprano voice of exceptional range and quality. Equally remarkable, and contributing to her fame, was the personal quality of Jenny Lind herself. Henry Wadsworth Longfellow, who attended eight of her Boston concerts and who met her on at least four occasions, testifies to the latter: "Her power is in her presence, which is magnetic." That power shone through her performance even though she sang "like the morning star; clear, liquid, heavenly sounds."[1] The person and the exquisite voice were so fused that one became the expression of the other. While residing in London in 1849, Lind abandoned the theater and her renowned operatic career to devote herself to concert and oratorio singing.[2]

While in London, Jenny Lind received an invitation from P. T. Barnum to make an extended American tour of 150 concerts to be arranged and managed by him. After negotiations, she accepted and arrived in New York Harbor on Sunday morning, September 1, 1850, to begin what Allan Kastrup has called "the most successful and influential tour of the United States ever made by a musical celebrity from Europe."[3] The welcome was elaborate and spectacular. A public relations campaign orchestrated by Barnum had prepared the American people for her coming. The first concert, at Castle Garden on September 11, was attended by seven thousand persons, the largest audience for which Lind had ever performed. She was accompanied by an entourage, the provision for which Barnum had arranged according to the terms of her contract. It included two of Jenny Lind's cousins—Miss Ahmansson, to serve as companion, and Max Hjortzberg, a secretary to manage her finances. Julius Benedict of Drury Lane Theater in London was engaged as musical director, pianist, and accompanist, and Giovanni Belletti as baritone soloist.[4] Shortly after Jenny Lind's arrival in New York, she was visited at her hotel, the Irving House on Broadway, by Olof Hedstrom and his associate Sven B. Newman.[5] They were warmly received and invited to attend a concert as her guests. In return, Lind later visited the Bethel Ship and became better acquainted with Hedstrom and his work. A pastoral relationship developed that made it natural for such meetings, at the singer's request, to conclude with prayer.[6]

Jenny Lind remained in the United States for twenty-one months, in the course of which she presented thirty-six concerts in New York City alone. Spangberg, in his account of Lind's career, states: "Jenny Lind was in the habit of attending church, whenever she could do' so without attracting notice. She always preserved her nationality, also, by inquiring for and attending Swedish churches, wherever they could be found."[7]

Her status as a highly visible celebrity must have been inhibiting. However, one day in 1851 she attended the service on the Bethel Ship and heard Hedstrom preach. Lind then followed Hedstrom into his office, and during the ensuing conversation, discussed the matter of her relationship to God. Several indications would seem to reflect that at this period of her life Lind was involved with an inner spiritual struggle. At one point a tearful Jenny Lind fell to her knees and begged Hedstrom to pray for her. The matter of theatrical and operatic performance must have been a part of their conversation. A day or two later, Hedstrom received a letter from Lind expressing gratitude for his kindness to her. In it she revealed her decision never again to appear in theater or opera, but only on the concert stage.[8]

Kastrup explored the motivations that prompted her decision: "Since she always identified herself with the operatic parts she created, life on the stage had become too strenuous for her, but there were also religious reasons for her decision."[9] On further contemplation, one would suspect that these are not two reasons, but two aspects of one. We know of Lind's prior predisposition toward pietism. If, by nature, her personality was such that she had a compulsive need to identify with the role she performed, then portraying values contrary to her moral and spiritual principles would indeed have been painful. Yet it was undoubtedly that identification which had contributed to her reputation as the greatest opera star of her time.

Hedstrom shared the Methodist and general pietistic conviction of that era regarding the sinfulness of the theater. In 1833, as previously noted, he disdained an invitation in Hamburg, Germany, to attend a theatrical performance. In the kindly warmth of the charismatic Hedstrom, Jenny Lind, experiencing an almost incomparable adulation and acclaim in her triumphant American tour, found comfort and reassurance. After her visit with him, her troubled spirit found expression in a simple six-line verse, written in Swedish:

> There is no peace, ah no
> In any created good;
> It offers me no joy,
> But only anxious thoughts
> There is no rest for me, O God
> Until my soul finds peace in thee.[10]

Apparently, the 1849 decision was not too widely known. The reaction of an aroused world occurred after the visit with Hedstrom, and he was forced to share the burden of her decision. Witting writes: "And we remember the commotion, the embittered outcry, this soon to become public decision of Jenny Lind aroused, not merely in America, but even to a greater extent in Europe. The world furiously raged against religion, heaped scorn on [Hedstrom], deplored her; but she kept her promise, since from then on Jenny Lind never appeared as an actress, but only sang in concerts."[11]

The letter Olof Hedstrom received from Jenny Lind after her attendance of the Bethel Ship service and their private conversation in the pastor's office was one of several that she wrote to him. Two have survived and have been placed in Swedish Methodism's archives.[12] We include the full text of the letters as they reflect the pastoral relationship that developed between Jenny Lind and Hedstrom, and also her deep pietistic spirituality. The first of the two, written and sent from Niagara Falls, was a response to Olof Hedstrom's letter in which he informed Jenny Lind that a gift from an "American" had been entrusted for the purpose of delivery to her. No mention is made in Hedstrom's letter concerning the nature of the gift, but from other sources we can with reasonable certainty deduce its nature. In the work of the Bethel Ship, an important vehicle for evangelization among immigrants and seamen was the distribution of Bibles and religious tracts. Hedstrom had requested the assistance of the Methodist Missionary Society in importuning the American Bible Society to publish a bilingual Swedish-English edition of the New Testament. The annual report of the Missionary Society for 1851 includes the following statement: "It affords us much satisfaction to say that the application of the Board to the American Bible Society to print an edition of the New Testament in Swedish and English languages was promptly attended to and we now have this work in addition to numerous others as the fruit of this blessed organization."[13]

Sven B. Newman, in his autobiography, relates that Jenny Lind received a beautifully bound Swedish-English New Testament as a memento.[14] Though the donor is not recorded, it is reasonable to assume that the gift must have come from someone in the American Bible Society or the Missionary Society, who made the gift through the Bethel Ship and its pastor. Her letter follows:

CLIFTON HOUSE
NIAGARA FALLS
October 4, 1851

Honored Herr Pastor,

 I had the pleasure of receiving your letter of the 29th of Sept., in which you kindly informed me that you had received a gift intended for me, from an American. I really cannot understand why I should be the recipient of a gift, but since it has been entrusted to your care for delivery to me, the donor must have well wishes toward me, and therefore I should accept the gift.

I shall return to Europe in the Spring, God willing, and shall certainly visit New York before then—in all probability toward the Christmas season—and therefore I beg Herr Pastor to kindly hold on to the present under consideration, and above all things do not go to the trouble of taking two steps to place it in my hands, or sending it to me. It will be both safer and more convenient to receive it from Herr Pastor when I arrive in New York.

Prior to Herr Pastor's letter, I had known that Herr Hemmerling had finished his earthly life and am thankful to God that his suffering is over. From all that I have heard concerning the deceased, he was not ignorant concerning the truth and the heavenly home. In my thoughts his widow is deserving of respect and sympathy. May she, and all of us comprehend the right significance of life and seek the true help in all troubles.

I have, praise God, not been ill, kind Herr Pastor, but have, and continue to feel perfectly well. It is quite common that exaggerated and untrue statements are made at my expense.

May God grant continuing success to Herr Pastor in his loving service to mankind. I confidently believe that Pastor's reward in the better world will be joyful and glorious.

With warm feelings and sincere esteem, I continue, my good Herr Pastor,

Your Humble Servant,

Jenny Lind

The second letter, written five months later, also needs to be placed in context. Dated March 1, 1852, it was sent from Round Hill, Northampton, Massachusetts, where Jenny Lind and Otto Goldschmidt were spending their honeymoon. Undoubtedly, her American tour had lasted longer than anticipated by Julius Benedict, the musical director, accompanist, and piano soloist. He resigned after a series of concerts given at numerous sites up the Mississippi and Ohio rivers to

Pittsburgh, and returned to England. Selected as Benedict's successor was Otto Goldschmidt, composer and pianist, from Hamburg, Germany, the son of a successful merchant. More important, he was a friend of Lind's—they had studied music together in Germany. On February 5, 1852, Jenny Lind and Otto Goldschmidt were united in marriage at a private home on Beacon Hill in Boston.[15]

Hedstrom had written a "very friendly" letter—obviously one of well wishes on her marriage. Lind's reply makes a significant contribution to our understanding of her inner spiritual life and some of the qualities of her husband. Hedstrom was a trusted friend, a confidant, a spiritual counselor, one to whom she could entrust her deepest thoughts and emotions and to whom she could comfortably turn for help and guidance. It would seem as though Jenny Lind was experiencing moments of distressing self-doubts. Hedstrom's letter had been a source of strength and reassurance. In her reply, she opens her soul and shares her plight with him.

Jenny Lind also assures Hedstrom that she had not forgotten the matter about which they had conversed during their last meeting. The *Henry Leeds* had been in poor condition when, in 1844, it was converted to a Bethel Ship. In 1851 it was dry-docked, caulked, repaired, and painted at a cost of forty-three hundred dollars. But this was a temporary expedient. Obviously, some alternative provision for the work of the Swedish bethel had to be made soon. This concern had been raised in the most-recent conversation between Hedstrom and Jenny Lind, and to which she now refers: "I hope we shall be able to contribute toward the fulfillment of Herr Pastor's further dreams of loving service for mankind." With these introductory statements as background, we include the entire letter.

NORTHAMPTON
Round Hill
March 2, 1852

Honored Herr Pastor,

It was with sincere pleasure that I received and read Herr

Pastor's very friendly letter. I felt myself strengthened by it and was grateful. Yes, surely our Divine Saviour is the very, very best to be found on this earth and for the life to come. Had I not believed that through marriage I would be in a school for spiritual training, and the hope that both I and he who belongs to me should be drawn to higher levels of life, I should in all probability remained unmarried.

The spirit is willing but the flesh is weak. I am inclined to feel miserable at times and so filled with sin that I hardly know how to pray. Kind pastor, do not forget me in your prayers.

My husband is a gifted and noble minded person. He strives for clarity and light, is fervent in spirit for the right and Divine truth. His mild disposition and temperament has already accomplished much good for me. I am very impatient and have many other faults, but God in his own good time will undoubtedly help me.

Herr Pastor must not think that I have entered the important stage of marriage without much contemplation. Oh no! I carefully pondered every aspect of the matter, and at every point received a clear inner conviction that I must act as I have.

I shall gladly give thought to ways in which I can render some service to my landsmen in America, and I beg Herr Pastor to have no misgivings concerning my sympathy with the important matter of a new church which Pastor mentioned when last we met. I shall consult with my new friend— my husband—and with good health next spring, before our return to Europe, I hope we shall be able to contribute toward the fulfillment of Herr Pastor's further dreams of loving service for mankind.

My husband, though unknown to you, sends his greetings, and also sincere regards from Mme Ahlmanson; and from myself the assurance of my highest esteem and devotion.

Respectfully, Herr Pastor's friend,

Jenny Goldschmidt
nee Lind

P.S. My warmest regards to Mrs. Hedstrom.

In the Hedstrom archival materials, we have one further item referring to Jenny Lind. The book in which Hedstrom wrote his truncated travel diary of 1833 had many remaining pages. In 1848, he began to use it to record marriages at which he officiated. When, in 1850, he received a share of a contribution Jenny Lind made to charitable causes, Hedstrom used pages to account for his stewardship.[16]

Jenny Lind understood her voice to be a gift from God, and with a sense of stewardship she found satisfaction in using her talent in the service of humankind. When P. T. Barnum made a farewell visit to Jenny Lind in her backstage room after her last American concert, she told him that she would not again sing in public. He reminded her that a good providence had endowed her with a voice that enabled her to contribute to the enjoyment and enrichment of her fellow beings. If she no longer needed the large sums that people were willing to pay to hear her sing, she knew by experience the pleasure she had received in devoting the money to the alleviation of human suffering. Her reply, in Barnum's words: "Ah, Mr. Barnum, that is very true; and it would be ungrateful of me not to continue to use, for the benefit of the poor and lowly, that gift which our Heavenly Father has so graciously bestowed upon me. Yes, I will continue to sing as long as my voice lasts, but it will be mostly for charitable objects, for I am thankful to say that I have all the money which I shall ever need."[17]

The day before the first concert after her arrival, held on September 11, 1850, when Jenny Lind heard that her share of the proceeds would be $10,000, she resolved to devote the entire amount to charity. She consulted Mayor Woodhull of New York, and with his advice her gift was distributed over a broad spectrum of community organizations. Several weeks later, on November 16, Lind appointed a committee to distribute $5,073.[18] The influence of Olof Hedstrom is evident in three items on the list:

Destitute children of seamen	$200
Swedes and Norwegians in New York	273
Swedish Bibles and Testaments	200

There is also a contribution of five hundred dollars to temperance societies. One suspects that here one finds the influence of the Swedish *läsare* movement. The accounting to which we have previously referred relates to the $273 designed for Swedes and Norwegians. The first page reads:

PAID ON ACCOUNT BY REV. O.G. HEDSTROM MONEY DESIGNATED BY COMMITTEE FROM JENNY LIND NOVEMBER 28th 1850

A stove for Swedish Deyer from Stockholm with Family very poor	$5.00
To Widow Wilson, a Swede for Clothing	5.00
A Poor Swedish emigrant—left in Gothenburg after his family came here destitute	1.50
A sick Norwegian baker—staying with Cabinetmaker Borkman	.50
A poor Swedish student lived at Landin's on charity	1.25
A sick Norwegian baker staying with cabinetmaker Borkman	.50
A Norwegian widow with several children for a months rent accompanied by Cabinetmaker Borkman's daughter	5.00
A Swedish girl—she lay sick at Widow Berglund—105 Greenwich Street	2.00
Mehel Blom, 103 Washington Street He is a Swedish emigrant with family	1.00
Overcoat and pants for A. N. Gnospelius A student from Stockholm—destitute	8.50

Olof Hedstrom was to discover that dispensing charity was not always an enviable task. When one day Hedstrom called on Jenny Lind at her hotel, she gave him six hundred dollars to be used either for the poor or for Bibles, at his discretion.

Possibly as a result of prior experience, to protect himself Hedstrom deposited the money with a well-known Swedish businessman whose office was located in the neighborhood of the Bethel Ship. The word soon got around that Lind had provided Hedstrom with a large sum of money for the poor. As a consequence, he was overrun by beggars and tramps. He sent them to Mr. Kindberg with an order that if they were found worthy of help, they could be given a small amount.[19]

Jenny Lind was a world celebrity before coming to the United States. The concert tour and the elaborate promotional efforts of P. T. Barnum assured a general awareness by the American public of her renown. Lind's interest in the Bethel Ship, her charitable gifts made through the Bethel Ship, and her pastoral contacts with Olof Hedstrom were well known. It was inevitable that Jenny Lind should become part of the Bethel Ship saga.

9

Jonas Hedstrom Migrates West

More Swedish immigrants settled in Illinois between 1845 and 1880 than in any other state in the Union. With those arriving in 1880, the scale for the first time was tipped in favor of Minnesota. The earlier pattern of Swedish immigrant settlement must be attributed to the presence in Illinois of Jonas Hedstrom. Oliver A. Lindner, a contributing editor of the four-volume *Swedish Element in America*, has written:

> Group after group of Swedish immigrants arrived at New York where they were first met by the elder Hedstrom, and with his knowledge of conditions in Illinois, acquired through his brother, he was in a position to recommend that region as a desirable place of settlement. And to those who followed his advice, Jonas Hedstrom at all times stood ready to offer assistance of all kinds. . . . And thus large numbers of Swedish immigrants came all the way from New York to Illinois, although tracts of good land were to be had much nearer. To the brothers Hedstrom there is due no small share of credit for the continued influx of Swedes into Illinois.[1]

Jonas Hedstrom was born in Nottebäck parish in Sweden on August 13, 1813.[2] At the age of fifteen he left home and resided on the island of Öland off the coast of southern Sweden in the Baltic Sea. In all probability, he was apprenticed to a blacksmith, whose trade provided Jonas's livelihood during his early years in America. We have previously recorded that, when Olof Hedstrom returned to New York from his missionary journey to Sweden in 1833, he was accompanied by two younger brothers, Jonas and Elias, the latter only seventeen years of age. During the trans-Atlantic voyage and a life-threatening storm, while Olof Hedstrom was conduct-ing a service, Jonas experienced a religious conversion.

There is an unfortunate paucity of information concerning Jonas Hedstrom in the four years between his recorded arrival in New York aboard the bark *Minerva* on October 17, 1833, and his arrival in Victoria, Illinois, in 1837. We do know that his stay in New York was said to have been brief. A previously referred to *Christian Advocate and Journal* article in January 1834, "The Love Feast and the Swede," states: "On his return passage one young man was converted to God and is now a member of a Class in this city."[3] Careful research reveals no listing of the name of Jonas Hedstrom in Method-ist class records. In those early days of his American sojourn, with no knowledge of English, or such limited knowledge as Olof could have imparted on their voyage to America, it would indeed be surprising if Jonas were more than a passive attendant at class meetings. On the other hand, the youngest brother, Elias, must have remained in New York for some time, since he is listed in 1834 as a member of the Tuesday evening class of the Second Street Methodist Episcopal Church.[4] He was later to become a successful cabinetmaker in Detroit, Michigan, where he was married in 1841. In 1850, it was re-corded that he was the father of two boys, Charles and Elias, and held $2,000 in real estate. He died February 10, 1855.[5]

There would seem to be no reason to question tradition, accepted by Victor Witting and other Swedish Methodist historians, that Jonas Hedstrom migrated to Pennsylvania, where he plied the trade of blacksmith. It will be recalled that Olof had spent a short time in Pennsylvania and had estab-lished a business there. During the period between his arrival in America and his migration to Illinois, two events, and by conjecture probably a third, were to have a direct influence upon the future life and career of Jonas Hedstrom.

At some point Jonas became acquainted with Diantha Sornberger and developed a romantic interest in her. To this, and indeed to the entire Sornberger family, we shall return in greater detail. A second incident led to the renewal and deepening of his spiritual commitment. The story is related by Witting in his autobiography and may well have been recounted to him by Jonas Hedstrom during his terminal illness in the late 1850s, along with many other details concerning his life. As friend, confidant, and pastor, Witting visited Hedstrom several times a week.

> [Following his emigration, Jonas] remained in New York a short while, after which he resided in Pennsylvania plying the trade of a blacksmith, learned in his homeland. This he did with great skill. In the meantime, the intensity of his spiritual life began to ebb, not in the sense of sin and worldliness—his conversion was too well grounded for that—but rather the spiritual flame no longer glowed as brightly. Attendance at prayer and class meetings seemed less urgent than before. In this precarious spiritual state, quite by accident, but in the providence of God, he overheard a conversation between two elderly, devout Christian women. They were speaking of the necessity for all who would love Jesus to live a holy life, demonstrated in words, manner of life, social relationship, and dress. They must withdraw from all worldly things, and live in devotion to Him whose life they shared by the shedding of his blood, and who redeemed them from their sins. The conversation stimulated his thought. The fading flame was re-ignited. With conversation of two godly women ringing in his ears, he resolved to wholeheartedly devote himself to the service of his Lord and Saviour. Henceforth, his motto would be "Holiness to the Lord."[6]

The third involves an assumption, one we shall later seek to justify, that between 1835 and 1837 Jonas Hedstrom visited and observed the work of his brother, Olof Hedstrom, then preaching in communities in the northern Catskill Mountains. When Jonas later began to hold services in small schoolhouses after his arrival in Illinois, it would well be in emulation of his brother, Olof.

An item from the Pennsylvania period relates to the Sornberger family. The historian writing in the last decade of the nineteenth century makes only an oblique reference to a romantic interest: "His [Jonas Hedstrom's] stay in Pennsylvania was terminated because the Sornberger family with whom he had become especially intimate, migrated west to Victoria, Illinois. Attracted by an invisible bond, he soon moved in the same direction."[7]

Because it was this family that accounted for Jonas Hedstrom's move to Illinois, with tremendous implications for a future development affecting Swedish immigrant settlement as well as the establishment of Swedish Methodism, it is imperative that we explore the Sornberger family.

George Sornberger, father of the large family, was born near Amenia, in Duchess County, New York, of German-speaking Alsace-Lorraine parents, on June 15, 1759. He had served in the Revolutionary War as a teamster in Colonel Roswell Hopkins's militia regiment of Duchess County. Sometime before 1782 he married Margaret Manson, and with her had six children. In 1799 he was married to Catharine Wolcott, with whom he had twelve children, ranging in age at the time of migration to Illinois from twenty to thirty-seven years. Diantha, the ninth child of the second family, was twenty-four. Three were deceased.[8]

The entire family had roots in the northwestern corner of Delaware County, New York, with some overlap of the boundaries of Otsego and Schoharie counties—in general, the Charlotte River valley. Diantha is said to have been born in Worcester, New York, just over the border in Otsego County. The Worcester town historian has confirmed that Diantha's older brother, Alexander, was overseer of highways in the two years prior to the migration west.[9] Several members of George's first family resided in Davenport, New York, in the southern portion of the Charlotte River valley.

It will be recalled that in 1835, when Olof Hedstrom was received as a traveling preacher in the New York Conference of the Methodist Church, his first appointment was to the Charlotte Circuit, with several Methodist classes and preaching stations up and down the Charlotte River valley.

The general assumption on the part of nineteenth-century Swedish Methodist historians has been that since Hedstrom lived in Pennsylvania, the Sornberger family must also have lived there. This seems clearly in error. There is no evidence that the family ever lived elsewhere than in the state of New York.

We have no knowledge of where in Pennsylvania Jonas had established his blacksmith shop, but assume it to have been in the eastern part of the state. Prior to his 1833 trip to Sweden, Olof Hedstrom had established a business in Pottsville, also in the eastern section of Pennsylvania. In view of their proximity, it would have been normal for Jonas to call on his brother. Circumstantial evidence would therefore suggest a strong probability of such a visit or visits, in the course of which Jonas and Diantha could have become acquainted.

On the surface, the Sornberger family's migration west in 1837 was somewhat unusual—George was seventy-eight years of age and Catharine, sixty-seven. The Kelly "Genealogical Survey" reports that all members of George's first family remained in New York and that George and Catharine were joined by ten members of their immediate family. Three of their twelve children were deceased, but Darius Olmstead, a son-in-law and widower of Electa, accompanied by their four children, filled the complement of ten. Two of the ten, Jane and Anson, did not immediately migrate with the family, but joined them later.

There had to have been some compelling circumstance responsible for uprooting George and Catharine from a well-established and comfortable home at their advanced age. The Illinois Territory was separated from the Northwest Territory in 1809 and became a state in 1818. After the War of 1812, the administration of the Illinois Territory designated the area between the Illinois and Mississippi rivers as a military tract for the benefit of soldiers.[10] War veteran George Sornberger would certainly have qualified for all intended benefits, and he and his family joined the stream of Eastern settlers following the conclusion of the Black Hawk War.

It was to Victoria, in Knox County, that the Sornberger clan came in 1837; they were soon followed by Jonas Hedstrom. The community had been established only two years earlier by a few pioneer settlers, who were predominantly Scottish in origin. It did not receive its name until 1837, when it was called Victoria in honor of the recently crowned queen of England. The population increased by a considerable percentage with the arrival of the Sornbergers. The earliest settlers of Victoria had chosen a location for their farms near a wooded area, where timber for their homes and wood for fuel were available. The village was later to expand into the open prairie.

The early history of Victoria is well documented.[11] In 1836 the community was visited by a Methodist preacher, Charles Bostwick. A justice of the peace and a constable were the first village officials, elected in 1837. The Sornberger family had brought several young children, undoubtedly contributing to the need for the first log schoolhouse, erected in 1838. It is also of interest to note that the first marriage in Victoria took place on Section 39, between Peter Sornberger and Phebe Wilbur on April 16, 1838. In succeeding years, members of the Sornberger family held positions of civic responsibilities in both the township and the village of Victoria. With the arrival of Swedish immigrants in considerable numbers beginning in 1846, one finds a generous sprinkling of Swedish surnames in the genealogical record of Sornberger descendants, indicating that other Swedes, following the example of Jonas Hedstrom, married into the family.[12]

Victoria apparently was not sufficiently large to support a profitable blacksmith shop. For this purpose, Hedstrom turned to the larger community of Farmington, Illinois, located thirty miles south of Victoria in Fulton County.[13] The skillful and energetic blacksmith began to lay the foundation of an economic security that would make possible full-time devotion to his missionary work among Swedish immigrants, with only modest subsidies from the Missionary Society of the Methodist Church.

The earliest available references to Jonas Hedstrom in Illinois, however, do not relate to blacksmith or business matters. They concern his religious activities in Methodist circles and his evolving leadership role in the Canton Circuit of the Rock Island District in Fulton County. He had natural gifts as a public speaker, and beyond that, a passion for the conversion of souls which subordinated any timidity caused by language limitations. Hedstrom was early given an exhorter's license and, in 1838, within a year of his arrival in Illinois, was awarded a local preacher's license. It was renewed at a Quarterly Conference of the Canton Circuit, held August 29, 1839, and countersigned by presiding elder (district superintendent) Henry Summers.[14] Evidence suggests that Hedstrom used his authorization assiduously, preaching in schoolhouses of surrounding communities.

A few days prior to the Quarterly Conference of the Canton Circuit, on August 17, 1839, Jonas Hedstrom and Diantha Sornberger were united in marriage by the Reverend Elijah Knox in Victoria. They made their first home in Farmington, where Jonas continued his work as a blacksmith and a preacher. Their first child, Almina C., was born there on October 12, 1840.[15]

Sometime during the course of the next year, the Hedstroms moved from Farmington to Victoria, where they were to remain permanently. Obviously, this had been their original intention, for in the summer of 1839 Jonas made his first real estate purchase—ten acres in Victoria Township, outside the village, for twenty-seven dollars. Their second child, Margaret Ann, was born in Victoria on January 6, 1842. The family was later increased with two more daughters and a son—Jane, Mary Charlotte, and George Luther, born, respectively, in 1844, 1851, and 1853.[16]

On moving to Victoria, Hedstrom joined two other entrepreneurs, John Becker and C. F. Reynolds, in creating the nucleus of the village of Victoria, described by J. W. Temple as "a store, a tavern, and a blacksmith shop."[17] The time came when the village needed to plan for expansion. The stagecoach route from Burlington to Chicago ran over the rolling prairie about one and a half miles northwest of the old town site, the direction in which Jonas Hedstrom had purchased his property. In May 1849, at the request of Becker, Reynolds, Hedstrom, and six other Victoria residents, a new village was plotted by the county surveyor, A. A. Denny. It became the present village of Victoria. Measured by standards of the time, Jonas built a substantial and comfortable home, which is still in use well over a hundred years later. It served as a hospice for many weary Swedish immigrants during the ensuing years.

No adequate portrayal of the life and service of Jonas Hedstrom can be made without recognition of his sound practical judgment in temporal matters. In addition to operating his shop, which produced plows, other farm implements, and wagons for the pioneer settlers, he became active in profitable real estate transactions. When he died in 1859, Hedstrom left an estate of six thousand dollars—not an inconsiderable amount in those days. His financial security and comfortable circumstances reflected the fulfillment of the "American Dream" and was therefore a source of encouragement to many immigrants. Thoroughly Americanized, Hedstrom was imbued with the principle of private enterprise, which brought him in direct conflict with the Eric Janssonists, who were to arrive from Sweden committed to a communal society. The contrast between Hedstrom's affluence and the squalid conditions of the early Bishop Hill colony unquestionably raised doubts in the minds of many who deserted, hoping to duplicate Hedstrom's success.

Jonas Hedstrom's practical business acumen was exceedingly helpful to the immigrants who arrived unfamiliar with both the language and customs of America. His guidance and counsel were important factors in their acculturation. In the development of Swedish Methodism, including the acquisition of church properties and buildings, Hedstrom's practical administrative skills supported his talents in spiritual and evangelical leadership.

When Jonas Hedstrom moved his home and business to Victoria, he also transferred his evangelical work to that area. He preached in neighboring schoolhouses, reaching out as far as Lafayette and Knoxville. In the early summer of 1845, Jonas received a letter with a New York City postmark from his brother, Olof. The elder Hedstrom told his brother of his new appointment to the Bethel Ship, ministering to Scandinavian sailors and immigrants. Thus, Jonas received his first intimation of the direction his preaching and ministry could take.

Shortly before his death, Jonas told Witting of his reaction to the 1845 letter. Witting, the meticulous and faithful diarist, wrote the account in the first person:

> When my brother told me that he had begun to preach in Swedish, and that in addition the Lord had already wonderfully blessed his work with the conversion of many souls, and that further he thought a large immigration from Sweden to America could be expected—the thought came forcefully to my mind; I must seriously try to recover the use of my mother tongue, for who knows if God is not preparing a similar work for me in this area. So one day I asked Brother Clark [a prominent preacher in the Rock River Conference] if he could tell me where I might purchase an English-Swedish Bible, explaining that I wished to refresh my ability to use my native language. Brother Clark looked at me and asked, "What good would that do you? There are no Swedes around here with whom to converse, and indeed no indication that any shall come." I answered, yes that is true, there are no Swedes here now—but something tells me that they shall soon arrive, and if this should happen, I would not want to be incapable of serving them.[18]

In August 1848, two years after the first Swedish arrivals, Jonas became a ministerial member on trial in the Rock River Conference of the Methodist Episcopal Church. In due course he was admitted to full membership and on August 21, 1850, was ordained an elder by Bishop L. L. Hamlin.[19]

Defections from the Bishop Hill commune provided Olof Hedstrom his first opportunity for Methodist work among Swedish people. In the autumn of 1846, only weeks after arrival in Bishop Hill, Janssonists were in Lafayette, organized into a Methodist class by Jonas Hedstrom.[20]

Other Swedes had settled in Victoria, where on December 15, 1846, Jonas Hedstrom preached his first Swedish sermon to a congregation of five persons, including Peter Newberg, whom Hedstrom had employed in his blacksmith shop and who later became a Methodist preacher. This group grew larger in the following two weeks. Around Christmas, they were officially organized as a Swedish Methodist church, the first in the Midwest and the first after the Bethel Ship.[21]

The trail blazed by the Janssonists to the Illinois prairie was followed by large numbers of persons from rural Sweden. Word of fertile and cheap land was quickly and widely circulated by press and private letters. The Hedstrom brothers, Olof in New York and Jonas in Illinois, were eager to be of assistance in their respective locations. Soon, Jonas Hedstrom surrendered his blacksmith shop for an itinerant ministry.[22] He arrived in communities almost simultaneously with the immigrants. His assistance in temporal matters was accompanied by an evangelical concern for their spiritual welfare—the new arrivals were sheep without a shepherd. Hedstrom gathered the little clusters of immigrants and formed Methodist classes, to which he rendered pastoral care. As each grew in number, it was organized into a church by Hedstrom in collaboration with the regional presiding elder. When, in 1848, Jonas Hedstrom was made a ministerial member on trial in the Rock River Conference and ordained a deacon, he could report Swedish Methodist churches in Lafayette, Victoria, Galesburg, Andover, Rock Island, Moline, and New Sweden in Iowa.[23]

Jonas Hedstrom possessed considerable administrative skills along with his business acumen and passion for the salvation of souls. The Methodist circuit system was advantageously used. His appointment by the bishop to the Swedish mission was indeed to a circuit, and Hedstrom was a circuit rider.

He surrounded himself with a coterie of young men whom he judged to have "gifts, graces, and usefulness." Andrew Ericson had been at work among the *läsare* in Sweden. Peter Newberg, Peter Challman, and Eric Shogren were early defectors from the Janssonists in Bishop Hill. The latter two were exceptionally able and eloquent. Since they all lived in or near Victoria, Hedstrom had easy access to them for training and administration. In the 1850s, persons with high intellectual and spiritual qualifications joined the ranks of Swedish Methodist ministers. Victor Witting, A. J. Anderson, Albert Ericson, and N. O. Westergreen would become leaders during the remainder of the nineteenth century.[24]

By 1856, Methodism among the expanding Swedish communities had developed to the point where a more manageable structure was considered essential. Swedish churches in Illinois, western Indiana, and lower Iowa were placed in a separate district within the Peoria Conference, and Jonas Hedstrom was appointed the presiding elder.[25]

The constant travel in severe and rugged conditions began to take its toll. Broken in health, Hedstrom was forced to withdraw from active work.[26] His last public appearance was at a Swedish district camp meeting held at Andover in the summer of 1857. Surrounded by ten pastors on the platform and a large representative congregation from practically all the churches of the district, from Chicago to Iowa, Jonas Hedstrom gave an unforgettable farewell address to an emotionally charged audience.[27] He lingered for almost two years, during which the pastor of the Victoria church, Victor Witting, was a constant friend and companion. Jonas Hedstrom died on May 11, 1859, at the age of forty-six. At his request, W. G. Graves conducted a memorial service in the American Methodist Church of Victoria, with Witting preaching the following Sunday in the Swedish church on Hedstrom's favorite text—John 3:16.[28]

In evaluating the life and work of Jonas Hedstrom, we must recognize his strong faith and total commitment. He was compassionate and eager to assist persons in need. He was extremely well-endowed with good sense and judgment. He had a sharp mind and was an able debater and administrator. There is considerable testimony concerning his preaching, which at times was quite eloquent. The young men whom he trained for work on the circuit and for admission to the conference offered anecdotes concerning his helpful suggestions.

Doctrinally, Hedstrom was much more polemic than his brother, Olof. Some have made much of his conflict with Lars P. Esbjörn, the Lutheran pastor with *läsare* sympathies who came to Illinois in 1849 to work among Swedes of his denomination. Hedstrom had been at work among the Swedes for three years and had established several Swedish Methodist churches. Tension between the two men was inevitable, given the natural bias and stance of each. Esbjörn, the well-trained Lutheran pastor coming from a land with an established Lutheran church, had to assume that every Swedish immigrant was Lutheran. Hedstrom, who had become Americanized and committed to a free church society, further shared the bias of dissenters against the perceived spiritual sterility within the established church in Sweden. Basically, both were *läsare* and had more in common than separated them. Their two religious cultures were in conflict.

10

Bishop Hill and Victor Witting

The Bethel Ship *John Wesley* and the Bishop Hill colony in Henry County, Illinois, are undoubtedly the two most colorful institutions of Swedish immigrant history in the nineteenth century. The saga of Bishop Hill and its founder, Eric Jansson, has been told in well-documented histories.[1] The scope of this work does not require elaborate detail concerning it. We must, however, deal with direct and tangential relationships between the two institutions, their leaders, and followers. Each seemed destined to affect the other in several significant ways. The unfolding story will note that Swedish Methodism was, in no small measure, indebted to the Janssonists.

Eric Jansson and his followers had no practical alternative other than flight to America. The leader and members of the sect were subjected to persecution, harassment, imprisonment, and sometimes life-threatening violence. An extreme and erratic form of pietism was confronted by institutional religious intolerance.[2] Official and legal proscription against religious activities apart from the established Lutheran church by the conventicle edict of 1726 would not be modified until 1860. In addition to legal restraints, the edict had fostered a cultural mindset that took many decades to change. Growing tolerance toward the *läsare* was noticeable, but far from general. There was some stigma attached to religious dissent for a long period.

Jansson was seen by substantial elements as egregiously provocative. Among his eccentricities were messianic pretensions, always supported by a liberal number of Biblical quotations with little or no regard to their context. His hostility toward the Lutheran church and his disdain for the conventional *läsare* movement were publicly proclaimed in book-burning demonstrations.[3] Flames devoured the works of Luther and other spiritual giants, including devotional literature revered by *läsare* pietists. In general, the vocabulary of the pietists, from which the Janssonists parted, was retained, but the meaning was drastically distorted. An example would be the Wesleyan concept of Christian perfection and sanctification, introduced to Sweden by George Scott.[4]

The Eric Janssonists were not without some defenders in high places. Chief among these was Lars Vilhelm Henschen,[5] a prominent jurist with *läsare* sympathies. An ardent foe of the conventicle edict, he entered the fray on the side of religious freedom. When the Janssonists were called before the Cathedral Chapter in Uppsala, the confession and defense offered was prepared by Henschen. As they moved through court appearances they had his counsel and guidance. Henschen admired America and its constitutional freedoms. He advised emigration when violence and public uproar reached intolerable dimensions. In some instances, parish priests created obstacles by denying exit visas for travel. Henschen opened the door for appearance before the king, who removed the obstructions. It should be noted in this connection that the Henschen name holds a place of honor in Swedish Methodist history. The brilliant son of the jurist William Henschen came to America and became the intellectual leader of the immigrant church. He received a doctorate in philosophy from Uppsala University in Sweden at the early age of twenty-one and served Swedish Methodism in America as a teacher and president of its theological seminary and as the editor of its weekly journal, *Sändebudet*. Between 1885 and 1899 Henschen held similar posts in the Methodist Church in Sweden.[6]

In the winter of 1845–46, Eric Jansson traveled surreptitiously across Sweden to Norway, much of it on skis and in considerable discomfort. He was accompanied by Lars Gabrielsson, a close associate. Given temporary hospice in Nor-

way, he was soon joined by his family. A farewell letter to his
followers in Sweden contained the prayer list to which we have
previously referred and assured them of a reunion in America. Eric Jansson was provided with a false passport, which
had originally been issued to Mr. and Mrs. Eric Larson, who
had been aboard the ill-fated *Ceres* and who had returned
home after their rescue.[7]

Jonas Hedstrom's premonition concerning the arrival of
Swedes was about to be realized. In the summer and fall of
1846, Swedes began to arrive in New York aboard cargo ships.
At the close of the year, four hundred Swedish immigrants
had settled at Bishop Hill in Illinois. Earlier, in the spring of
1846, Olof Olsson arrived in Victoria with a letter of introduction and commendation from Olof Hedstrom to his brother. Olsson was Eric Jansson's emissary, commissioned to search
out suitable land on which to establish a religious commune.

The blacksmith Jonas Hedstrom and the farmer Olof Olsson
quickly established a firm rapport. Both shared a strong
interest in religion and spoke a common language and idiom.
Before becoming caught up in Eric Jansson's form of pietism,
Olsson, together with his brother, Jonas, had been community leaders in the *läsare* movement. As such they had traveled
to Stockholm on several occasions and became acquainted
with the Methodist George Scott, whose influence on Swedish religious life was widespread. With faded trousers tucked
into his boots to protect against the spring mud, Hedstrom,
accompanied by his new friend, trudged over the prairies
inspecting farm sites. Olsson was impressed with the rich,
deep loam of the Illinois prairie. He made a hasty explora-
tory trip to Wisconsin and Minnesota and returned convinced that the colony should be established in Illinois. In
addition to the fertile soil, the presence of an experienced,
knowledgeable, and bilingual Swede who was eager to help
must also have added weight to the decision. Olsson sent for
his family, who were still on the Bethel Ship. They moved into
a log cabin on land owned by Hedstrom. The purchase of
property had to await the arrival of Eric Jansson.

Olsson was not idle in the meantime. He arrived in Illinois, as noted, with a favorable opinion of Methodism and the Bethel Ship program, indicated to family and friends in his letter of December 31, 1845. Enticed also by lush land at reasonable cost, Olof Olsson privately purchased forty acres of farmland, preparatory to separation from the Janssonists. On his own land, he began to till the soil.[8]

Eric Jansson and his family arrived in New York in late March or early April, and stayed there longer than anticipated. The stressful circumstances under which they left Sweden, in addition to the long, arduous journey, must have been extremely difficult for Maria Kristina, who was pregnant. In New York, she gave birth to a stillborn child.

Following a period of missionary work in New York, Jansson traveled to Victoria in early July, with Maria Kristina and their two children, Eric and Mathilda. They shared Hedstrom's log cabin with the Olsson family. Eight persons crowded the small cabin under the best of circumstances, but the tension became intolerable when Jansson discovered that Olsson had become a Methodist and had privately purchased property. Jansson's son Eric recalled years later the theological battle that raged at breakfast, dinner, and supper. He hid under a blanket one night when the more physically powerful Olsson threatened to throw Jansson out of the cabin. In the morning, he was relieved to see that the two men were still speaking.[9]

The Janssons were accompanied by four additional persons on their trip west. Two were women from Falun who, according to Paul Elmen, author of *Wheat Flour Messiah*, had traveled with them from Sweden. The other two were Sophia Pollock and her American husband, identified only as Mr. Pollock. The scant evidence available leaves little doubt that Mr. Pollock was George B. Pollock, a member of the Asbury Society which purchased the *John Wesley* in May 1845. When, in July, a meeting was called over the signature of O. G. Hedstrom for the purpose of providing a corporate structure for the work of the Bethel Ship, Pollock was one of a small group of laypersons present. He was elected secretary and signed the resolution that became part of the charter and certificate of incorporation for the North River Bethel Society of the Methodist Episcopal Church. *The New York City Directory* for 1845 and for 1846 identifies George B. Pollock as a clerk, 70 Wall Street, and his residence as 460 Greenwich Avenue. His name does not appear in the 1847 edition.[10]

Sophia Pollock was a foundling in Gothenburg. At the age of fifteen, in 1832, she came to New York with her foster parents; she subsequently married a seaman who never returned from a voyage. Under the influence of Hedstrom, Sophia became a member of the Bethel Ship congregation and thus met Pollock. She attended Jansson's meetings in New York, and persuaded by him was determined to accompany him to Illinois. Elmen sums up the unfortunate consequences for her husband: "Pollock had gone along very reluctantly. The difficult circumstances of frontier living among a people with a strange culture and language and a religious expression he did not understand were too heavy a burden. It was said that he died of a broken heart."[11] Sophia married twice more, the last time to Eric Jansson himself shortly after Maria Kristina died in the cholera epidemic of 1849.

With the arrival of Eric Jansson, purchase of property for the colony could now proceed. Hedstrom's assistance is reflected in the quick, successive acquisition of three parcels of land.[12] On August 1, 1846, sixty acres of land located on the crest of a low hill were purchased at Red Oak Grove in Henry County, sixteen miles north of Victoria. The cost was $250. Signing the documents of purchase on behalf of the Eric Janssonists was Olof Olsson. Some have assumed that his collaboration indicated reconciliation; others have noted that Olsson continued to live on his own land. Sometime that month, Eric Jansson and his family moved to Red Oak Grove.

Approximately thirty days after the first purchase, a fifty-six-acre farm equipped with a building, livestock, and grain was acquired at neighboring Hopal Grove at a cost of eleven hundred dollars. On September 26, 428 acres of government-owned land was purchased at $1.25 per acre.[13] Of the four hundred residents at the end of the year, seventy lived at Red Oak Grove and the remainder lived at Hopal Grove. The colony was named Bishop Hill, an exact translation of *Biskop-skulla*, Eric Jansson's birthplace in Uppland, Sweden. Living conditions were crude, as would be expected in any pioneer venture of the period. The Janssonists, industrious and committed, developed their community rapidly but not without sacrifice and deprivation.

The first contingent of Eric Janssonists to attempt emigration was aboard the *Ceres*, wrecked in a storm while still in Swedish waters. The incident, now a footnote to the travail associated with Janssonist immigation to America, became an important event in the history of Swedish Methodism in both America and Sweden. Victor Witting was a member of the crew — possibly a junior officer. A few months earlier, he had completed studies at the Malmö School of Navigation and had taken the first mate examination. Witting admitted that it was the demeanor of young Janssonists during a life-threatening situation so severe that all hope of survival had faded which changed the direction of his life. He later was to become one of the legendary figures of Swedish Methodism, which he was to serve as pastor, editor of *Sändebudet* (Messenger), missionary to Sweden for the purpose of structuring institutional Methodism, and Swedish Methodism's prime historian. Prior to going to sea, Witting had been educated at Malmö Latin Skola and Landskrona Elementarläroverket.[14] In addition, he had studied to be a pharmacist, which stood him in good stead later in life. To Witting we are indebted for a graphic portrayal of the *Ceres* catastrophe.

Shortly after Olof Olsson had been dispatched to America, the first group of sixteen or seventeen Eric Janssonists boarded ship at Gävle in October 1845, bound for America.[15] First they sailed north in the Baltic Sea to Söderhamn for a cargo of iron. Before long they were overtaken by a violent storm. Blinding rain and snow, wind-driven waves crashing over the ship's deck, iron cargo torn loose and shifting in the hold, a lone sailor who dared venture out on the deck dismembered by a flying object—such were the horrific scenes aboard the *Ceres*. With severely reefed sail, the captain sought cover at Öregrund, hoping to cast anchor, but the erratic movement of the ship had caused the anchor chain to become entangled. At about eight-thirty in the evening, the ship was lifted by a giant wave and tossed onto a barren island of huge rocks. The bow, with forecastle, was wedged between two rugged cliffs. The stern and quarterdeck parted and immediately sank.

Crew and passengers crowded into the forecastle. All expected the remaining portion of the ship to be splintered by the pounding sea. In contrast to the natural violence without and the emotional turmoil among the crew were the courage, serenity, and faith displayed by the Janssonists, especially the young. With tender concern, they moved among the distraught seafaring men as they sat or lay upon cots. At midnight, the Janssonists celebrated the Lord's Supper, never expecting the dawn of another day. Some crew members participated, among them Witting, an admitted agnostic only a few hours earlier. When rescued at noon the next day after the rough sea had subsided sufficiently for boat launching at the shore, Witting vowed that he would see the Janssonists again.[16]

The *Ceres* disaster did not deter other Janssonist adherents from the difficult and dangerous voyage. Within a relatively short time the population of Bishop Hill reached twelve hundred. But not all who set out for the colony reached their destination. Some died on the long ocean voyage, others did not survive the rugged trip westward from New York. The schooner *Betty Catherina* left Söderhamn on August 8, 1846, with sixty Janssonists aboard and disappeared without a trace.[17]

Many of the new arrivals were physically debilitated after the long and difficult travel. Cargo-carrying vessels had few amenities for passenger travel, and the ocean passage required six to eight weeks—sometimes longer. The trip west in overcrowded canal boats and ships plying the Great Lakes added another stressful three weeks. It was not uncommon for a ship to pull along some deserted shore to permit a relative or friend to dig a shallow grave for a loved one. Arriving at Bishop Hill, immigrants found provisions minimal, so it is not surprising that some new arrivals became disenchanted. Defections began to occur almost from the outset. When they did leave the colony, the Janssonist immigrants almost invariably turned to Jonas Hedstrom in Victoria for guidance and assistance. Witting states that in the period between 1846 and 1848, several hundred persons left Bishop Hill and settled in surrounding communities. The earliest came to Victoria and Lafayette, where Hedstrom could help secure employment. Before Christmas of 1846, for example, Peter Newberg, later to become a Methodist preacher, was at work in Hedstrom's blacksmith shop.[18] Several were employed in Lafayette, helped by successful entrepreneur Jonathan Hodgson. Jonas Hedstrom maintained contact with the immigrant community. Every week he traveled to Bishop Hill with medicines and other necessities. He often brought back ill persons in his carriage to be cared for in his home.

In a bitter but somewhat ambivalent complaint, Eric Jansson's son years later accused Jonas Hedstrom of being responsible for the defections. However, in the same statement he also gratefully acknowledged the humanitarian services Hedstrom rendered at times of great distress. There is no doubt about Hedstrom's aversion to a communal society where persons lived on the verge of poverty when ample land was cheap and opportunity for independent living available. Nor did he have much sympathy for Jansson's expression of pietism.

Though a frequent visitor to Bishop Hill, Jonas Hedstrom appeared there publicly only once for a scheduled debate with Eric Jansson. That visit clearly defines the adversarial relationship of the two men. In all probability the affair was initiated by Hedstrom. Swedish Methodist historians described the truncated event: "Jansson spoke first and directed attention to his unique and divinely appointed status, for which he found ample support in specific scriptural passages. Hedstrom sought to interpret the meaning and context of the cited scripture, much to Jansson's annoyance. He became angry and abusive toward Hedstrom. Even some Janssonists thought it went too far and showed their displeasure by withdrawing."[19]

The cholera epidemic struck Bishop Hill in July 1849.[20] Several Norwegians previously converted to Janssonism arrived after having been infected on their journey. One hundred forty-three colonists died within a six-week period. Bishop Hill was devastated. Frightened people from neighboring communities challenged Jansson's dependence on faith for protection and threatened to notify the authorities if he failed to call in a physician. Dr. Robert D. Foster, whose services the prophet reluctantly engaged, was not much of a physician—Unonius considered him a charlatan. He exploited the hard-pressed and economically naive Jansson by charging staggering fees. When the sums could not be paid, Foster demanded signed notes encumbering the property. Bishop Hill barely escaped financial ruin. Victor Witting, with his pharmaceutical training, was pressed into service as assistant to the doctor. His autobiography records the catastrophe.

Following the wreck of the *Ceres*, Witting had encountered the Janssonists a second time while in Stockholm seeking work as a seaman. He learned that a brig was about to sail for New York and applied for a job with its crew, only to discover the last place had been filled a day earlier. But here again the Janssonists were to play a fortuitous role, with consequences for Witting's future career. Some Janssonist adherents were passengers aboard the brig. They had been consulted by the captain about securing a person with experience at sea to serve as a steward to care for their needs. When the Janssonists learned that Witting had been aboard the *Ceres*, the question was readily settled. They sailed into New York in October 1847. Witting describes their continuing journey: "Since I had won their good will on the passage and also they were probably hopeful of my conversion to the 'prophet,' they offered me a free trip from New York to Illinois and urged my acceptance. Because I wanted to travel inland, and also remembered my promise to seek out these folk, a promise made on that frightful night, the invitation was accepted with pleasure."[21]

Witting's arrival in Bishop Hill was delayed until the summer of 1848 because of illness and an extended period of hospitalization in Chicago, followed by employment in a pharmacy. He remained in Bishop Hill for about a year and a half. The stay was rewarding, though he was never an ideological Janssonist and did not consider himself a member of the commune. He had, however, profound respect for their deep sincerity and faith.

Witting found a life companion in Bishop Hill, a blessing for which he was eternally grateful. On September 12, 1849, Victor Witting and Catharina Lind were united in marriage in Bishop Hill. Catharina was born in Bollnäs parish, in the province of Hälsingland, Sweden, on March 14, 1830, the child of Olof Lind and Anna Greta Dahlström. They were adherents of the Janssonists and in 1846 decided to join the general exodus of that sect to America. They set sail from Gävle aboard the bark *New York*, which arrived in New York Harbor on March 20, 1847. The passage had been stormy and dangerous. One daughter, Anna, died and was buried at sea. Shortly before reaching the harbor, Anna Greta also perished, followed soon after by a second child, possibly Lena Greta, approximately four months old.

Little wonder that the distraught and bereaved father returned to his native land at the earliest opportunity. Olof Lind had lost heart for any further travel. Catharina, seventeen years old and devoted to her newfound faith, continued west to Bishop Hill with like-minded young friends of the company from Sweden. Two years later, when Catharina married Victor Witting, she had become disillusioned with Janssonist doctrines and practice.[22]

With the approval of his bride, Witting set out for Victoria and Jonas Hedstrom on Christmas Eve, 1849. On Christmas

morning he attended *Julotta* service in a private home, his
first Methodist meeting since attending a service on the
Bethel Ship conducted by Olof Hedstrom. (The following
day, Witting accompanied Jonas Hedstrom to Galesburg,
where Hedstrom was certain he could assist him in securing
employment with Lamphere's pharmacy.) A small Swedish
Methodist church had been established, with services twice a
month conducted by Jonas Hedstrom in a schoolhouse and
weekly class meetings under lay leadership. On March 20,
1850, Victor and Catharina, together with Eric Shogren, also
to become a Swedish Methodist minister, joined the Methodist church.

Witting's *Minnen Från Mitt Liv* (*Memories from My Life*)
began as a personal account. It soon developed into a history
of Swedish Methodism, which established Witting as the
prime historian of this segment of Swedish immigrant history. Beyond his youth and early life in America, he recorded
little of his personal and family life. From a memorial address
by Henry Emanuel Whyman, Witting's successor as pastor of
the Quinsigamond Church in Worcester, Massachusetts, and
Catharina Witting's pastor during the last years of her life, we
learn that she had been the mother of eleven children and
was survived by nine children and fifteen grandchildren, in
addition to her husband and a sister. She died in Worcester on
September 10, 1901.

The memoirs, in addition to providing biographical data,
speak of her gentle nature, clear thought and sound judgment, great capacity for friendship, and rich voice and musical talent. She had contributed, in no small way, to the
production of collections of hymns and songs, edited by
Victor Witting and widely used throughout Swedish Methodism.[23]

Victor Witting encountered Olof Hedstrom a second time
when, after an eventful but unfruitful expedition for California gold, he had spent a season growing medicinal herbs
which he took to New York in expectation of a higher market
price. Instead he found that the bottom had fallen out of the

market. He received only enough to pay the freight and sundry expenses, with nothing remaining for travel back to Illinois. In a state of deep depression, Witting was taken to New Year's Eve and New Year services at Madison Street Methodist Church by his hosts, Mr. and Mrs. Oberg, members of the Bethel Ship congregation. Here he surrendered his life to God, and the next morning went to Hedstrom and the Bethel Ship. Counseling continued for several days until Hedstrom secured funds for Witting's homeward journey to Illinois. On arrival, Witting began taking a leadership role in worship and proclamation of the Gospel at services and meetings.[24]

11

From Ship to Scandinavian Shores

The Bethel Ship *John Wesley* was firmly moored and secured with strong chains to Pier 11 on the North River—its sailing days over. But the words proclaimed from its pulpit traveled widely. Someone once said that the best way to send a message is to wrap it up in a person—and the Bethel Ship message was wrapped up in people whose lives had been transformed. Westward their witness spread throughout the states, primarily to midwestern communities where these immigrants settled. It was also carried eastward across the Atlantic to Scandinavia, to inland towns and villages to which sailors and an occasional returning immigrant came to relate how their conversion had changed their lives and attitudes. In the process, incipient awakenings often stirred entire communities.

As reports of these awakenings filtered back to the Bethel Ship, generally through correspondence with Olof Hedstrom, they were shared with his coworkers. Reporting to the Missionary Society of the Methodist Episcopal Church, Hedstrom said, "Several of our brethren, seamen, and others, have been moved by the good Spirit of God to go home to their native land and warn their friends to flee the wrath to come, and the Lord has blessed their labors."[1] In a more extensive report, as the movement increased in intensity, Hedstrom wrote, "These are our epistles; sailors converted to God at the Bethel Ship, scattered over the seas and read and known of all men. . . . They go as Paul the tentmaker to carry the glad tidings of salvation in Christ. . . . May our Bethel Ship become the spiritual birthplace of a thousand souls."[2]

The Missionary Society saw this development as a fortuitous extension of the work of the Bethel Ship, with which it had been involved since the beginning:

> Doubtless the primary motive which led these foreigners to seek our shores was to improve their worldly condition; but it was equally clear that God intends to make this outgoing from the old to the new world, a powerful means of restoring evangelical religion to the nations on the continent of Europe. . . . From the converts among them . . . living missionaries have not so much occasion to carry back the doctrines of Christianity as to carry back the life of evangelical religion.[3]

The *läsare* movement, which had been enormously enhanced and expanded by the charismatic George Scott, had been continued by his successor Carl O. Rosenius. From Hedstrom and the Bethel Ship now another kindred influence fed into the larger stream of Swedish pietism. Though in the beginning there was no other thrust than the conversion of souls and the promotion of an awakened and revitalized spiritual life, eventually the Bethel Ship influence was to lead to the development of a free church denomination, separated from the established Lutheran church and organizationally related to American Methodism. Two factors made this possible: financial support and encouragement from America, and the liberalization of laws restricting religious freedom in Sweden. The first can be attributed to Hedstrom's role and influence with the Methodist Missionary Society. His intervention was generally by request from individuals and groups in Scandinavia. The seeds of religious freedom and free church separation were always inherent in the *läsare*, as well as in pietism in general. The largest free church in Sweden, the Mission Friends, later the Mission Covenant, nonetheless never withdrew from the established church.

Who were Hedstrom's "epistles" who returned to awaken relatives and friends? Among those whose names have been recorded were August Olson and Bengt Borjeson, who worked in their hometowns in the province of Halland. Their colorful mate, Jöns Lindelius, after his conversion on the Bethel Ship, was employed as a colporteur by the American Seaman's Friend Society, in New York, briefly in London, and finally on his native island of Gotland. Others from Gotland were C. Levander and J. Lindquist. Jonas Östlund returned to Hälsingland and B. A. Carlson to Dalsland.[4] A. M. Graezen, living in Brooklyn and very active in the Bethel Ship congregation, several years later moved back with his family to Örebro, in the province of Närke.

Graezen invited Victor Witting to hold a service there in the chapel of Carolinska Realskolan. This first Methodist service conducted in Sweden was attended by an overflow audience on September 15, 1872, and marked the establishment of a strong congregation.[5] In Denmark, the first Methodist service was conducted by the sailor Boje Smith; and in Finland, Gustaf Lervik and Gustaf Barnlund bore their Bethel Ship witness.[6]

We have reserved for more extended treatment four major personalities in the history of Methodism in the Scandinavian countries: John Peter Larsson, the first designated Methodist missionary to Sweden, whose career covered the remainder of the nineteenth century; Ole Peter Petersen, the founder of Norwegian Methodism; Christian B. Willerup, the founder of Danish Methodism; and Victor Witting, whose leadership was a major factor in establishing the Methodist Conference in Sweden.

Shipwrecked on his way back to Sweden in 1852, John Peter Larsson and his shipmates were rescued by a British ship and carried to Sweden. Larsson had been converted on the Bethel Ship under the preaching of Olof Hedstrom in 1851. He had remained in New York long enough to have been active in the services and programs of the Bethel Ship. When he arrived at his home in Lotahammar, in the province of Småland, he began to tell neighbors and friends about his religious experiences in America. Eighteen months later, he wrote a letter seeking counsel from Olof Hedstrom, which in turn prompted the following letter from Hedstrom, dated September 14, 1854, to the corresponding secretary of the Missionary Society of the Methodist Church:

> I have recently received a letter from one of our members now in Sweden under very interesting circumstances, and apparently by direct appointment of Divine providence. . . . With the Divine blessing, [Larsson has] awakened so great a religious interest that he has been detained [in Lotahammar] for more than eighteen months. "Working with his own hands" meantime to support himself. The longer he stays the more difficult he finds it to leave, and now he seeks advice from me as to whether he shall remain, and if so, how he shall work, etc., etc.
>
> My judgment is, if he should remain, and act as colporteur for us at present, until we shall see what the providence of God shall open to us. In order to have him remain, I think it necessary that an appropriation of $200. per annum be made for his support. In all probability, before another twelve months shall have passed, we have need to send a missionary to that Country.[7]

The letter was presented to the appropriate committee, the request was approved, and the grant made—the first financial subsidy granted by the Missionary Society for work in Sweden. The society received a letter from Larsson dated November 18 of that year. In it he reported the expansion of his mission to the city of Kalmar and described the nature of his work with distressed families and with people disturbed by their past sins and in need of forgiveness, and distribution of tracts and Bibles. The following year, Larsson was included in the list of appointed missionaries with the designation "missionary–Sweden." The records of the Methodist Missionary Society gave 1854 as the beginning of the Scandinavian mission.

That Larsson's work was effective is confirmed by S. M. Swenson, a Bethel Ship class leader and one of its more affluent members. In June 1855, he went to meet Larsson at Kalmar and became immediately involved in evangelistic work.

Spending six days with his friend, he learned that Larsson was held in high esteem by his Christian friends. A letter sent from Sweden to Olof Hedstrom suggested that the attention fixed upon them by the "high and learned" was due in part to the fact that they "spoke the word of God as laymen only":

> Brother Larsson and I went on from morning until night to visit from house to house, and we had from three to four meetings a day. I was about to start for home several times, and ordered my horse, but was pressed by the people to stop one day after another. Large salons were filled with people of all classes. Several clergymen, magistrates, school teachers, and other learned men were present, and before these brother Larsson and I had to stand and declare the word of God. I hope it was not in vain.[8]

Later, when the Sweden Conference was organized, Larsson was one of its leading ministerial members, serving for a time as superintendent.

A special relationship developed between Olof Hedstrom and Ole Peter Petersen, a Norwegian. Petersen arrived in America in January 1844 and apparently sailed the Atlantic coastal shipping lanes for the next five years. While in New York, he became acquainted with the Norwegian John Harris and his Swedish wife and stayed at their home. On his second New York visit, he learned that the Harris family had become "new creatures." He accompanied his hosts to the Bethel Ship and heard Hedstrom preach. On one such occasion, Petersen responded to an altar call but was only able to say, "I thank God because I have had the opportunity to be here today, for tomorrow we sail. I am determined to seek God until I find him." It was not until 1849 that he had a sense of God's presence in his life, though his shipmates, playing upon his first name, called him "Holy Peter."

Before leaving Norway, Petersen had become engaged to Anna Marie Amundsen, and he wrote her a letter describing his conversion. Her response illustrates the power of innumerable similar testimonial letters in the promotion of religious awakening.

> Dear unforgettable friend! After a long time of waiting I have received your dear letter, which I have read over and over again under tears and with great wonder over what God has done for you. Many of my friends have read it and I have lent it out so it goes almost from house to house in the town and out in the country. Many of my friends join in this prayer: Do come home as soon as you can, take us by the hand and lead us unto that path you have found.[9]

Bishop Odd Hagen has stated that when Petersen returned after five years, Fredrikstad was ripe for a revival.[10] His testimony in the homes of that city bore fruit. On April 24, 1850, Petersen, with his bride, sailed for America. On his arrival in New York, Hedstrom convinced Petersen that he was called to be a preacher. Shortly thereafter, Petersen was appointed an assistant to Hedstrom by the Missionary Society. Having received a local preacher's license in 1851, Petersen was assigned to work among Norwegians in Iowa.

In the meantime, Hedstrom was receiving strong appeals from those in Norway who had come under Petersen's influence during his brief stay in Fredrikstad. They urged that someone be sent to nurture and carry on the revival. Official records of the Missionary Society report:

> At a meeting of the Foreign German Committee of the Mission held March 16, 1853, Pastor Hedstrom called attention to this revival in Norway, begotten of the visit of Mr. Petersen, and a special committee was raised by the Board to bring the subject before the Bishops having charge of foreign missions. The Committee promptly discharged their duty, and on the 8th of June following, Bishop Waugh addressed a letter to Mr. Petersen, recalling him from Iowa, and directing to report to the Corresponding Society as a Missionary to Norway. His business, as the Bishop told him, was "to raise a people for God" in Norway.[11]

On July 31, 1853, Petersen was ordained both a deacon and an elder by Bishop Beverly Waugh, who then made the appointment official. Petersen and his family arrived later that year and settled in Sarpsborg, outside of Fredrikstad, where he developed a congregation that was organized in 1856 as the first Methodist church in Norway (laws affecting free churches had been liberalized in that country in 1845, much earlier than in Sweden).[12] Petersen later returned to America and served as pastor in charge of the Bethel Ship in the early 1860s when Hedstrom was forced to take a leave of absence for health reasons.

Christian B. Willerup was something of an anomaly. The son of a wealthy Copenhagen family in Denmark, he came to America when he was very young and at age seventeen taught school in Savannah, Georgia. He experienced conversion, joined the Methodist Episcopal Church, and was eventually made a local preacher. After a year back in Denmark, during which he married, he returned to America and settled in Stroudsburg, Pennsylvania, where he was successful in business. His pastor had a large circuit, and Willerup was soon involved in assisting him. Willerup was ordained a local deacon and in time was recommended for the traveling ministry by the Philadelphia Conference. As he was about to become a probationary member of the Genesee Conference, someone, in all probability Olof Hedstrom, deeply concerned about the need for Scandinavian ministers among Norwegians and Danes in Wisconsin, brought him to New York. After consultation, Willerup was ordained an elder on the Bethel Ship by Bishop Edmund S. Janes, transferred to the Wisconsin Conference, and appointed to missionary work among Norwegians and Danes.[13] Extremely gifted, he was later made superintendent of Methodist work in the Scandinavian countries, and except for a brief period in Norway, lived and worked in Denmark. Assisted by Boje Smith, Willerup became the founder of the Methodist church in Denmark.

Methodist work in Sweden developed more slowly than in neighboring Norway and Denmark. As noted, Ole Peter

Petersen was appointed to work in Norway as early as 1853. In 1856, Christian Willerup was appointed to work in Norway and Denmark. He remained in Norway and established a congregation in Halden. Willerup returned to his native Denmark in 1858 with the assignment to become a general and active evangelist in Copenhagen. In due course, Willerup was appointed superintendent for the Scandinavian Mission.[14] His natural interests in Norway and Denmark preoccupied him. Hedstrom felt it his duty to remind Willerup of his responsibilities toward Sweden, as well.

It was not until 1867 that Methodist work in Sweden was given the attention it deserved. In 1868, superintendents for each of the three countries were appointed—Willerup in Denmark, Petersen in Norway, and Victor Witting in Sweden. The 1867 annual report of the Missionary Society made this statement with reference to the Sweden Mission: "There is a more general awakening among the people, and in some places particularly in Stockholm and gottenburg [*sic*], and in their vicinities, this awakening is widespread and profound. . . . The mission in Sweden has been greatly strengthened by the transfer of Rev. V. Witting to Sweden this year, and God has raised two or three powerful young men to help in this part of the work."[15]

Victor Witting was one of the ablest pastors of Swedish Methodism in the nineteenth century (see Chapter 10 for an earlier discussion of Witting's role in midwestern Swedish Methodism). "Methodism in Sweden—the Lord's Hand in the Matter" is the title given to the chapter in which Witting records the events, including his own involvement, in the development of Methodism in his native land.[16] The fortuitous circumstances surrounding his travel to Sweden and its subsequent consequences were, to him, amazing and providential. One May morning in 1867 a Mr. Johnson, engaged in the lumber business, walked into the *Sändebudet* office in Chicago and asked Witting—its editor and a casual acquaintance—if he would like to accompany him as a traveling companion on a trip to Sweden with expenses paid. In this fashion Witting was able to fulfill a long-dreamed-of wish to visit his aged father and his native land. He arrived in Gothenburg the week before midsummer and immediately looked up his old friend, John Peter Larsson, engaged in missionary work in that city. Witting was invited to preach on a Wednesday evening. He then parted from Mr. Johnson, who was headed for Norrland, and traveled south to Skåne, where his relatives resided. He preached on several occasions in Malmö, his hometown, and also in Lund, where a mission chapel was gladly made available. The attendance increased with each service and included many students and members of the general church of Sweden.[17]

On a visit to Copenhagen to see the new stately Methodist church about which he had read, Witting met Bishop Calvin Kingsley, who was on an episcopal tour of Methodist missions. The bishop had heard of the awakening in Stockholm, the result of preaching by Albert Ericson, and invited Witting to meet the bishop and Willerup at Benikebrinken Hall in Stockholm.[18]

Albert Ericson had left Stockholm for his home in America on May 1, the day that Mr. Johnson had entered Witting's office in Chicago. Swedish Methodists in America had voted to establish a Swedish Methodist Episcopal Theological Seminary and had elected the well-educated Ericson to teach Swedish language and literature. To prepare himself, Ericson went to Sweden to study at Uppsala University. While there, he was invited to preach at a Baptist chapel. Rumors concerning his excellent sermon and the fact that he was a Methodist preacher quickly spread. George Scott was still remembered. Several persons with immigrant relatives had learned through correspondence about Methodists and were eager to hear more. They invited Ericson to preach in Stockholm and rented Benikebrinken Hall.[19] Within a short time the powerful and eloquent preacher had an overflow audience. The adjoining room was soon filled, as was the lobby and stairwell—even the street was crowded. In order to guarantee a seat, some were known to take a lunch and remain from the morning service until the evening service. Many who attended were converted, dissatisfied as they were with the Lutheran Church, finding the colporteurs among Mission Friends inadequate, and disagreeing with the Baptist point of view. Gathered around Ericson was a group of exceptional young persons, several of whom became Methodist ministers and leaders in the Sweden Conference and Swedish Methodism in America. Two should be noted: Johan Kihlstrom, who had been converted in 1834 through Rosenius and was thus a part of Scott's program; and Daniel S. Sorlin, who served in America.[20]

This was the congregation to which Bishop Kingsley, Christian Willerup, and Victor Witting came in the early summer of 1867. Requests had been made to retain Ericson in Sweden and when an affirmative answer arrived from America, Ericson had already departed. Bishop Kingsley preached at a service, translated by Willerup; Witting also preached on several occasions. The bishop invited Witting to remain in Sweden, which he said he would like to do but for his obligations to *Sändebudet* and to his family in America. The bishop responded that he would take care of arrangements for *Sändebudet*, and that Witting should go to America for the purpose of relocating his family to Sweden. Thus began a new era for Methodism in that Scandinavian country.[21]

Four years earlier, in 1863, Olof Hedstrom had made a four-month visit to Sweden while recuperating from a breakdown in health brought on by eighteen years of labor on the Bethel Ship. Whether or not he intended it, his trip had become intensely missionary in nature. In a letter dated July 23, 1863, Hedstrom described his activities:

> I am now near the city of Carlscrona, Sweden, at the house of the widow of my deceased brother, and just in time to assist her to settle the estate. I cannot describe the hunger and thirst with which all people here desire the Word of God preached to them. You may judge for yourself, when I tell you that I have preached fourteen times in two weeks. Many of the people have come from ten to twenty-five, and in some cases even forty English miles. I have preached five times in a large

mission house in the city of Carlscrona, but the crowd was so great that the people had to stand, and it was with great difficulty I could press my way through into the house. The yard and surrounding houses were filled also, so we opened the windows and the hymns were sung as distinctly in the yard as in the house. Immediately upon entering the city the news spread abroad, so that in less than an hour I would have a large congregation, even on the week days, of all classes of persons, some of high rank as officers too, and some of low. Having an invitation I went out some eighteen miles to Ronneby—the Saratoga Springs of Sweden—where there are hundreds of persons taking the mineral waters. I preached to a great multitude of these, who drank in the word with all readiness. The great mass of the people pressed about me at the close, sending forward the most influential of their company to entreat me to preach to them again, and this was done time and again, so that after preaching to them three times I was obliged to tear myself away; and yet I am constantly beset by numbers who are coming and going wherever I am known to be, so that I can scarcely find time to write these lines. I leave this place tomorrow by steamer for Carlshamn, where I expect to preach, a telegram having been sent to that effect. From that point I go to Malmö and Copenhagen. From Copenhagen I go with Brother Willerup to Gottenberg [sic], Sweden, and from thence to visit all our missions in Norway. You perceive that I have work enough on my hand; may the Lord help me for Christ's sake. I see plainly that the burden I have for many years had upon my heart to visit my native land was of the Lord. I fear that I shall be carried late into the Year before I can leave for America. My health has been very good, though I have been travelling or preaching constantly since my arrival. I have received invitations to visit and preach in the cities of Stockholm, Gottenberg [sic], and Gefle. I doubt if my time and means will allow of all this, and yet I shall try. Dr. M'Clintock insisted that I should visit Paris before leaving Europe. God has wonderfully sustained me in my work, and I have had uninterrupted spiritual comfort.[22]

To the Swedish public, Olof Hedstrom was a person of considerable stature. His extraordinary efforts on behalf of

Scandinavian immigrants and the impact of his religious ministry were well known. Invited to preach in an established church one day Hedstrom was offered the privilege of conducting the entire service, including the Lutheran liturgy. He demurred, and the pastor agreed to be the liturgist if Hedstrom would preach the sermon. The pastor became so absorbed in Hedstrom's message that he forgot to move to the chancel to read the prayers and the usual announcements. Hedstrom interpreted the Gospel as offering full and free salvation from sin, to be accompanied by holy and righteous living, for "where is it written that a man shall ultimately come to God burdened with the baggage of a multitude of sins?" Hedstrom's preaching in Sweden had an enduring influence.[23]

In 1867, Dr. John P. Durbin, the corresponding secretary of the Missionary Society, visited the Scandinavian countries. He wrote in the annual report:

> During my visit to the Scandinavian work, I formed the opinion, that if Brother O. G. Hedstrom could be spared from his own work in America, he ought to go as an evangelist to Scandinavia at least three months each year or four months every two years, and go from city to city, and from town to town, rousing the people, and thus begin the work which the brethren would preserve and extend in the intervals of Brother Hedstrom's visits.[24]

The suggestion was never implemented. Victor Witting's appointment to the superintendency of the Swedish mission in a letter from Durbin dated April 14, 1868, made it unnecessary.[25] Witting was more than qualified for the task. Blessed with the advantages of an upper-middle-class upbringing, he was well educated. Witting was an excellent preacher, a compassionate evangelical, and a good organizer. Under his leadership, Methodism ceased to be a scattered movement, becoming instead an institution.

One of Witting's first duties as superintendent was to go to Karlskrona to organize forty of Hedstrom's converts in that city, and thirteen in neighboring Nättraby, into a Methodist society, as the congregations were called.[26] He had previously organized the Gothenburg society in January 1868, one week after the first Methodist society had organized in Stockholm. The Gothenburg work was also a product of Hedstrom's initial preaching. Others were to follow in rapid succession— Walda and Släp in Halland, Kalmar, and Visby.

The first meeting of Methodist preachers was called by Witting on September 17–24, 1868, in Stockholm. Seven preachers were present: Witting, John Peter Larsson, Alex Palm, Seved Hansson, Erik Carlsson, Johan Kihlstrom, and Daniel S. Sorlin.[27] This group formally organized the Swedish Methodist Mission Society with a constitution and bylaws enabling it to function as a conference in American Methodism. They met annually, heard reports, planned the program of expansion, and assigned preachers to locations and societies. Important among their decisions was the establishment of a publishing house and a Methodist monthly publication to begin January, 1869, and to be named *Lila Sändebudet*, thus relating it to *Sändebudet*, the journal established in America.[28]

The religious environment in Sweden was rapidly changing to the advantage of the dissenters and the free-church movement, in spite of the fact that there was still considerable harassment and even persecution of Methodists in some areas as late as 1868 and after. However, in 1873 the Swedish administration put before Parliament the new Dissenter Law, which was enacted with minor protective modifications.[29] The law made it possible for dissenters to withdraw from the established church which they did not attend and with which they had theological differences. The Methodists, at their annual meeting of the Methodist Mission Society, decided to take advantage of the Dissenter Law by petitioning that the Methodist Episcopal Church be recognized as a free and independent denomination.

A deputation consisting of ten ministers and laypersons under the leadership of Victor Witting was appointed. They asked for and were granted an audience with King Oscar II in

February 1875. The deputation appeared with a petition signed by twelve hundred persons and the appropriate documents attesting to their withdrawal from the state church. Copies of the Methodist Episcopal Church's *Book of Discipline* (which included the Articles of Religion, the structure of the denomination, and its form of administration), the psalmbook, the catechism, and a copy of John Wesley's sermons were presented to the king.

King Oscar's cordial reception put the members of the deputation at ease. He asked each his name and place of residence, and assured them that they should feel free to express themselves in all matters. After Witting had presented the petition and briefly commented upon it, King Oscar observed, "I cannot give you an immediate and definite promise, but I shall do whatever I can for you." There followed an extended and apparently amiable conversation. Finally, the king asked, "But what is the basic difference between you and the Lutherans?" Witting's answer, "Primarily in the doctrine of the sacraments and holiness," seemed to surprise him. The king further inquired, "Holiness? What then is the difference?" His question demanded a full explanation:

> We believe that a person is made righteous by grace through faith in Christ, and his mercy alone. In addition, this new life of grace can only be maintained and developed through a continuing faith. If it is a true and living faith, according to our understanding of God's word, one receives power and strength to live a holy life. The lesson taught through grace leads not only to the forsaking of ungodliness and worldly lusts, but also disciplined and righteous living in the world, for which faith in Christ serves to provide the needed power. According to our view, Holiness means that a person is *in reality* saved through the blood of Christ and made free from all sin—and that one loves God with a clean heart, and his neighbor as himself. Such a condition we believe to be every person's privileged right, and it was just for such a purpose that God's Son came into the world and died upon the cross

for our sake. But in spite of all this, the true Christian, the holy person, can have many shortcomings and faults and to the extent they become apparent through the working of God's Spirit, the Christian must make his confession and repent.[30]

The king listened carefully and then commented, "That we all have shortcomings—that must be acknowledged. But what about Baptism and Holy Communion?" To which the answer was given: "With reference to these, we approach the *Reformed* position."

The monarch asked if Methodists baptized children. Responding to an affirmative answer, he said, "That is good." Continuing, he stated that as the *Summus Episcopus* of the Church of Sweden he could do nothing that would offend or undermine that church, as the deputation would understand, but, "I have heard nothing but good about you and I shall do whatever I can."

At that point A. Sandell, a former officer in the Kalmar Regiment, assured Oscar II that Methodists, unlike some dissenters who denied their military obligations, were always ready to hazard their lives for king and country. Johan Kihlstrom, in the same spirit, indicated that their motto was "Fear God and honor the king." The monarch then raised his hand and said, "God be with you my people! God be with you my people!" and stepped into an adjoining room. Witting called their audience "one of the most joyous and blessed days of my life."[31]

A year later, on March 10, 1876, after clearance by all the cathedral chapters in the Episcopal Dioceses of Sweden, a resolution granted official status to the Methodist Episcopal Church with authorization of its ordained clergy to officiate at marriages, burials, and other pastoral duties in conformity with the law. The resolution contained the names of the ten petitioners and listed twenty-nine Methodist Episcopal congregations.[32]

12

An Accomplished Mission

The Bethel Ship mission in its original form ended on August 12, 1876. On that day, the chains that had secured the *John Wesley* to Pier 11 on the North River were released and the ship was gently towed across New York Harbor. It was moored at the foot of Harrison Street in Brooklyn to serve as a chapel for Norwegian Bethel Ship members who were residing in that community. In 1879 the ship was again moved, this time to Jersey City, New Jersey, where for several years it served as a chapel for Erie Canal boatmen. On October 31, 1890, the following announcement was made in the *New York Tribune*: "The old Bethel Ship *John Wesley* which for many years had been used for mission work on Fifteenth Street and was patronized by boatmen principally, was sold yesterday at auction for $295.15. This included the altar, bell, and the old Bethel flag." Frank Dahnson, one of the last Bethel Ship survivors, reported that the *John Wesley* was moved upstream and left to disintegrate.[1]

Olof Gustaf Hedstrom, after a rigorous and demanding forty-year ministry for the Methodist Episcopal Church, laid aside his burden and retired to Cape May, New Jersey, in 1875. As Methodist ministers continue to be full members of the conference from which they retired, Hedstrom planned to attend the 1877 annual session of the New York Conference. Invited to be a guest at the home of Albert Chellberg, an old Bethel Ship member, Olof Hedstrom arrived on March 13 for an extended nostalgic visit to New York City. While with the Chellbergs, he became ill and died several weeks later on May 5. Services were conducted at St. Paul's Methodist Episcopal Church, to which Hedstrom had been officially related throughout his Bethel Ship years. The memorial sermon was preached by Lucius H. King, a longtime friend and colleague. Hedstrom was buried in Greenwood Cemetery in Brooklyn. Swedish Methodists gathered at the grave nine years later to dedicate a monument memorializing Olof Gustaf Hedstrom, the founder of Swedish Methodism. A biographical address was delivered by the Reverend Holger Olson, who had assisted Hedstrom on the Bethel Ship shortly before Hedstrom retired.

In the process of dissolving, the Bethel Ship congregation gave birth to three strong and vibrant churches, each proud of its origins. The Immanuel Swedish Methodist Church was built under the auspices of the North River Bethel Society in cooperation with Brooklyn Bethel Ship Swedish members. It was dedicated on Sunday, May 19, 1872. Hedstrom had secured substantial contributions from supportive benefactors. Still in existence, it operates under the original Bethel Ship charter, amended only to change the name. Two years later, in 1874, the Reverend Ole Peter Petersen, associated with Hedstrom for many years (see chapter 11), organized a small group of Bethel Ship Norwegians living in Brooklyn—it was to accommodate them that the *John Wesley* was moved to Brooklyn in 1876. The Norwegian congregation in 1879 acquired Mariners church in Brooklyn through a gift. They immediately changed its name to Bethelship Norwegian Methodist Episcopal Church. Also in 1874, some Bethel Ship members living in Manhattan began holding weeknight meetings in the uptown Rose Hill Methodist Church. After the removal of the Bethel Ship, they were technically members of the Immanuel Church and were ministered to by its pastor. On May 17, 1882, the Manhattan membership incorporated as the Swedish Methodist Episcopal Church in the City of New York. It became known as the Lexington Avenue Swedish Methodist Church.

It should be recorded that services to Scandinavian immigrants were not discontinued upon Hedstrom's retirement. A bilingual Swedish pastor designated as port missionary continued to be appointed as late as 1941, when the Eastern Swedish Conference of the Methodist Church was merged into geographically contiguous conferences. The port missionary's support was provided by the Methodist Board of Missions and the New York City Society. He was a counselor and guide to arriving Scandinavians, assisting in their entry process at Ellis Island and travel to their intended destination. Like his forebear, Olof Gustaf Hedstrom, the port missionary was indeed a pastor to the immigrant.

Notes
Index

Notes

Foreword

1. Lee Benson, *Turner and Beard: American Historical Writing Reconsidered* (Glencoe, Ill.: The Free Press, 1960), 82.
2. Wade Crawford Barclay, *History of Methodist Missions* (New York: The Board of Missions and Church Extension of the Methodist Church, 1949), 1:266–67.
3. Bishop Ole E. Borgen, "Olof Gustaf Hedstrom: Father of Scandinavian Methodism," *Historical Bulletin of the World* (Methodist Historical Society) 2 (1967):6–7.
4. Arlow W. Andersen, *The Salt of the Earth: A History of Norwegian-Danish Methodism in America* (Nashville: Parthenon Press, 1962).
5. Henry C. Whyman, "The Conflict and Adjustment of Two Religious Cultures as Found in the Swede's Relation to American Methodism" (Ph.D. diss., New York University, 1937). Available from University Microfilm International.

1. The Unintentional Immigrant

1. Victor Witting, *Minnen Från Mitt Liv* (Worcester, Mass.: Burbank & Co. Tryckeri, 1904), 137–39. Witting quotes from Harold Wieselgren, *Vår Samtid*, 63–65. Also, Carl Thunstrom, *Olof Gustaf Hedstrom: Den Svenska Metodismens Fader* (Stockholm: Nya Bokförlag Aktiebolaget, 1935), 101–2.
2. Witting, *Minnen*, 138.
3. Ibid., 139; Sven B. Newman, *Sjelfbiografi* (Chicago: Svenska Metodist Boklådans Förlag, 1890), 77.
4. Nottebäck parish records, Sweden. Biographical materials were researched by Wesley M. Westerberg.

5. Carl-Erik Johansson, *Cradled in Sweden* (Logan, Utah: Everton Publisher, 1972), 117.

6. Olof Gustaf Hedstrom, travel diary, Swedish Methodist Collection, Drew University, Madison, N.J.

7. Nils William Olsson, *Swedish Passenger Arrivals in New York, 1820–1850* (Chicago: Swedish Pioneer Historical Society, 1967), 13.

8. While living in Sweden, the Hedstroms spelled their surname with the umlaut (Hedström). Following immigration to America, the umlaut was omitted. We have followed the latter practice throughout this book.

9. Obituary, *New York Times*, May 7, 1877, p. 8, col. 4.

10. Most Methodist sources give the date of marriage as June 11, 1829. The same sources also state that Hedstrom was converted two weeks after the wedding. Church records establish March 28, 1829, as the date Olof and Caroline Hedstrom enrolled in a class in the Second Street Methodist Episcopal Church. Holger Olson gives the January 11, 1829, date of marriage in an address in the presence of Caroline Hedstrom and reported in the *Christian Advocate and Journal*, 62, no. 25 (June 23, 1887): 400.

11. A biographical sketch of Caroline Hedstrom can be found in the A. J. Anderson Papers, Swedish Methodist Collection, Drew University.

12. Methodist church records, Manuscript Room, New York Public Library.

13. Samuel A. Seaman, *Annals of New York Methodism: Being a History of the Methodist Episcopal Church in the City of New York from A.D. 1766 to A.D. 1890* (New York: Hunt and Eaton, 1892), 265.

14. Witting, *Minnen*, 139.

15. The A. J. Anderson Papers.

16. "The Love Feast and the Swede," *Christian Advocate and Journal*, 8, no. 20 (January 10, 1834): 77.

17. *Methodist Membership and Other Official Records*, vols. 79–82, New York Public Library.

18. Abel Stevens, *History of the Methodist Church*, 4 vols. (New York, 1867), 2:114–15.

19. Witting, *Minnen*, 140.

20. Seaman, *Annals*, 199.

21. F. Ernest Stoeffler, *Continental Pietism and Early American Christianity* (Grand Rapids, Mich.: Erdman, 1976), 218.

22. Carroll Smith Rosenberg, *Religion and the Rise of the American City: The New York City Mission Movement, 1812–1870* (Ithaca, N.Y.: Cornell Univ. Press, 1971), 86–89.

23. Sydney E. Ahlstrom, *A Religious History of the American People*, 2 vols. (Garden City, N.Y.: Doubleday, 1975), 1:558.

24. Ibid., 1:557. "From the first he [Finney] demanded that some kind of relevant social action follow the sinner's conversion." Rosenberg (*Religion and the Rise of the American City*, 69) quoting Finney: "I want you as fast as you learn anything on the subject of revivals, to put it into practice and go to work and see if you cannot promote a revival among other sinners."

25. Witting, *Minnen*, 140; N. M. Liljegren, N. O. Westergreen, and C. G. Wallenius, *Svenska Metodismen i Amerika* (Chicago: Svenska M. E. Bokhandels-Föreningens Förlag, 1895), 153.

26. Witting, *Minnen*, 139.

27. Newman, *Sjelfbiografi*, 76.

28. Stevens, *History*, 4:288–95.

29. Seaman, *Annals*, 253–54.

30. *Christian Advocate and Journal* 35, no. 13 (March 29, 1860): 52. The article recounts a revival at Ashland Institute. Wilbur was among the converts. It is of interest that John Burroughs, the naturalist, attended Ashland Collegiate Institute earlier, according to his biographer Clara Barrus.

31. Ibid., 37, no. 27 (July 3, 1862): 216.

32. Ibid., 15, no. 39 (May 12, 1841).

2. Steps Toward the Methodist Ministry

1. Hedstrom, diary.
2. Ibid.
3. Ibid.
4. Ibid.
5. Ibid.
6. Ibid.
7. Ibid.
8. Ibid.

9. Olsson, *Swedish Passenger Arrivals in New York*, 12–13.

10. "The Love Feast," 77.

11. Ibid.

12. Olsson, *Swedish Passenger Arrivals in New York*, 12.

13. "The Love Feast," 77.

14. Methodist church records, New York Public Library.

15. *Doctrine and Discipline in the Methodist Episcopal Church* (New York, 1832), 32.

16. Methodist church records, New York Public Library.

17. David L. Watson, *The Early Methodist Class Meeting: Its Origins and Significance* (Nashville: Discipline Resources, 1985), 100ff.

18. *New York Methodist Episcopal Conference Journal*, 1835.

19. Ibid., 1837.

20. Ibid., 1838.

3. The Circuit Rider

1. *New York Methodist Episcopal Conference Journal*, 1876. This journal is printed annually. The information is found under the rubric "Pastoral Record."

2. John Bangs, *Autobiography of John Bangs* (New York: Privately printed, 1846), 117–18.

3. Edward White, compiler of an undated pamphlet published in Walton, New York. The original is in the library of the Garrett-Evangelical Theological Seminary, Evanston, Ill.

4. Ibid., 32.

5. Heman Bangs, *The Autobiography and Journal of Rev. Heman Bangs* (New York, 1872), 29–30.

6. Elbert Osborn, *Autobiography* (New York: Privately printed, 1865), 59.

7. Ibid., 29–30.

8. Joseph Hartwell, "Chapters from Memory" no. 7. *Prattsville District Register*, 2, no. 12 (December 1885): 60.

9. Thomas W. Lamont, *My Boyhood in a Parsonage, New York* (New York: Harper Brothers, 1946), 95–96. William R. Phinney, *History of the Fergusonville Academy* (Stamford, N.Y.: Privately printed, 1970).

10. Phinney, *History of Fergusonville*. Minutes of the Charlotteville Circuit quarterly meetings, November 29, 1834, and Septem-

ber 12, 1835, New York Conference Commission on Archives and History, White Plains, N.Y.

11. *Wyoming Conference of the Methodist Church Journal* 1900. Memoir of Joseph Hartwell, 111–12.

12. Hartwell, "Chapters," 60–61.

13. Lamont, *My Boyhood*, 92–102. Minutes of the Jefferson Circuit quarterly meeting, February 20, 1836, New York Conference Commission on Archives and History.

14. Osborn, *Autobiography*, 62.

15. White, pamphlet, 32.

16. Osborn, *Autobiography*, 61–63.

17. Ibid., 75–76. "That week was a season of great mercy to the people of the Charlotteville. We had some ministerial help from abroad, and though it was a very busy season with the people of that place who were mostly farmers, yet evening after evening they collected in the church to hear the word of the Lord. The pious wife rejoiced with her repenting husband; and the Christian who had for seventeen years been praying for his father, saw that father bowing at the mourners bench, a place which he had once despised. The minister of the gospel, in one instance was called from his bed at night to pray with the mourner. The servant of the Lord warned the people 'publicly and from house to house.' It was thought that in the course of one week, about twenty persons in that neighborhood found peace in believing" (ibid).

18. Ibid., 72–75.

19. Ibid., 94.

20. Ibid., 95.

21. Daniel Steele, "Pastor Olof G. Hedstrom," *Stilla Stunder* 5 (1893): 269. While a student at Boston University School of Theology, C. G. Wallenius became acquainted with Steele and learned of his early association and indebtedness to Olof Hedstrom. In 1893, Wallenius asked Steele for his written recollections, which were then translated into Swedish and published that year in *Stilla Stunder*, a Swedish Methodist publication. Quoted in Witting's *Minnen*, it was, until my recent research, the only open window known to Swedish Methodist historians through which to view Hedstrom's ten-year ministry in the Catskill Mountains. The memoir on Steele is found in the *New England Conference Journal* (1915), 131.

22. Steele, "Pastor Olof G. Hedstrom."

23. Ibid.

4. Hedstrom's Relation to the Läsare

1. Ernst Newman, *Nordskånska Väckelserörelser under 1800 Talet* (Stockholm: Svenska Kyrkans Diakonistyrelsens Bokförlag, 1925), 25.

2. Ibid., 63.

3. Stoeffler, *Continental Pietism*, 9–12.

4. Gunnar Westin, *Ur Den Svenska Folkväckelsens Historia ock Tankevärld* (Stockholm: Evangeliska Fosterlands Stiftelsen Bokförlag, 1930), 19. Newman, *Nordskånska*, 98.

5. George M. Stephenson, *The Religious Aspects of Swedish Immigration* (Minneapolis: Univ. of Minnesota Press, 1932; reprinted by Arno Press and the New York Times, 1969), 24.

6. *An Encyclopedia of Religion*, ed. Vergilius Ferm (New York: The Philosophical Library, 1945), 506, 582, 730, 840.

7. Hilding Pleijel, *Hernhutismen i Sydsverige* (Stockholm: Diakonistyrelsens Bokförlag, 1925), 10–11.

8. Stephenson, *Religious Aspects*, 11.

9. Stoeffler, *Continental Pietism*, 186. Luke Tyerman, *The Life and Times of the Reverend Samuel Wesley* (London: Epworth Press, 1866); this volume documents a family trait of religious dissent.

10. John Wesley, *Christian Perfection as Believed and Taught by John Wesley*, ed. Thomas S. Kepler (Cleveland and New York: World Publishing Company, 1954), 3–4.

11. John Wesley, *Journal*, 1, May 24, 1738. Tyerman, *Life and Times of the Reverend Samuel Wesley*, 1:180.

12. Albert C. Outler, *John Wesley* (New York: Oxford Univ. Press, 1964), 15–16.

13. John E. Smith, *Jonathan Edwards: Religious Affections* (New Haven: Yale Univ. Press, 1959). Also quoted in the introduction, William Warren Sweet, *Revivalism in America* (New York, 1957).

14. *Letters of John Wesley*, ed. John Telford (London: Epworth Press, 1931), 1:154–55, 163.

15. Ibid., 1:179.

16. Mansfild Hurtig, ed., *Metodistkyrkan i Sverige 100 År 1868–1968* (Stockholm: Nya Bokförlags Aktiebolag, 1968), 12–13. J. M. Erikson, *Metodismen i Sverige* (Stockholm: K. J. Bolins Förlag), 8.

17. John Curtis Clay, *Annals of the Swedes on the Delaware*, 5th ed., with an introduction by Henry S. Henschen (Chicago: John Ericson Memorial Committee, 1938). Liljegren, Westergreen, and Wallenius, *Svenska Metodismen i Amerika*, 133–45; Amandus Johnson, "History of the Swedes in the Eastern States from the Earliest Time until 1782" in *Swedish Element in America*, 4 vols., ed. Erik G. Westman (Chicago, 1931), 2:1–59. Cf. Michael F. Metcalf, "Dr. Carl Magnus Wrangel and Prerevolutionary Pennsylvania Politics," *Swedish Pioneer Historical Quarterly* vol. 27, 1976.

18. *Journal of John Wesley*, ed. John Telford (London: Epworth Press, 1931).

19. *Letters of John Wesley*, 5:179, 5:302, 6:196.

20. Erikson, *Metodismen i Sverige*, 10–11.

21. Stephenson, *Religious Aspects*, 9, 12, 117.

22. Hurtig, *Metodistkyrkan i Sverige 100 År*, 14; Erikson, *Metodismen i Sverige*, 7–11.

23. Gunnar Westin, *George Scott och Hans Verksamhet i Sverige* (Stockholm: Svenska Kyrkans Diakonistyrelsens Bokförlag, 1929), 1:99.

24. Gunnar Westin, *Den Kristna Friförsamlingen i Norden, Frikyrklighetens uppkomst och utväckling* (Stockholm: Westerbergs Förlag, 1956), 68–69. Also, Stephenson, *Religious Aspects*, 26. To inform the Swedish public about Methodism, George Scott had published a sermon that he preached at the English chapel on February 13, 1833, titled, "Some Words about Wesleyan Methodism and Its Teaching." It was widely distributed. Westin stated: "During the great campaign against Scott 1841–1842, Methodist and *Läsare* were regarded as identical, and to be a committed Christian was considered by the secular press as being Methodist" (Westin, *Den Kristna*, 68–69).

25. Stephenson, *Religious Aspects*, 16.

26. Arthur Wilford Nagler, *Pietism and Methodism* (Nashville: Publishing House M. E. Church, South, 1918), 157.

27. Westin, *George Scott*, 519–38.

28. Ibid.

29. Gunnar Westin, *Ur den Svenska*, 1–26.

30. Evald B. Lawson, "The Origins of Swedish Religious Organizations in the United States with Special Reference to Olof Gustaf Hedstrom" (Th.D. diss., Biblical Seminary in New York, 1937), 8. Scott's American diary notations were made available to Lawson by Gunnar Westin.

31. George Scott, letter to the Missionary Society of the Methodist Episcopal Church, September 30, 1841.

32. Stephenson, *Religious Aspects*, 14–16.

33. Ibid., 19.

34. Stephenson, *Religious Aspects*, 15, 116. During the years George Scott preached in Sweden, he never favored separation from the state church and many years later he was critical of the work of American Methodism in Sweden. Gunnar Westin would differ in some respects. He believed that it was Scott's aim to establish a Methodist movement that would do for Sweden what Methodism did for England a century earlier. Westin, *George Scott*, 206–7, 229.

5. *Peter Bergner, Pioneer Missionary*

1. "North River Mission—Conversion of a Sailor," unsigned article, *Missionary Advocate* 2, no. 2 (May 1846): 13.

2. Sources concerning the Bethel Ship and its overall influence are numerous, including autobiographies and articles in Methodist and interdenominational journals. See in particular, Liljegren, Westergreen, and Wallenius, *Svenska Metodismen i Amerika*; Erikson, *Metodismen i Sverige*; Newman, *Sjelfbiografi*; J. M. Reid, *Missions and Missionary Society of the Methodist Episcopal Church*, 2 vols. (New York: Phillips and Hunt, 1879); and J. T. Gracey, *Missions and Missionary Society of the Methodist Episcopal Church*, 3 vols. (New York, 1895–96). The last is the work of Reid, revised and expanded.

3. Olsson, *Swedish Passenger Arrivals in New York*, 8.

4. Gracey, *Missions*, 2:181. The official arrival date was August 27, 1832. The date given by Gracey (August 26) could represent a flaw in Bergner's memory. There is always the possibility that the *Minerva* reached the harbor late on August 26 and that disembarkation occurred the next day.

5. Witting, *Minnen*, 152.

6. Nils William Olsson, *Swedish Passenger Arrivals in U.S. Ports* (St. Paul, Minn.: North Central Publishing Co., 1979) 86. Newman and Witting state that Bergner was born in the province of Jamtland.

7. Gracey, *Missions*, 2:180–81.

8. Newman, *Sjelfbiografi*, 82.

9. The dramatic story of Bergner's conversion is retold, almost in stereotype, in the sources in note 2, above, and in magazine articles too numerous to list.

10. Carroll Smith Rosenberg, *Religion and the Rise of the American City: The New York City Mission Movement 1812–1870* (Ithaca: Cornell University Press, 1971), 84ff.

11. *New York City Tract Society Annual Report for 1844*, in the office of the New York City Mission Society.

12. Reid, *Missions and Missionary Society*, 1:431. Gracey, *Missions*, 2:181.

13. Witting, *Minnen*, 154, claims there were twenty-eight Scandinavian vessels in New York Harbor at the same time. The date is not given.

14. Ibid., 148. See also Lawson, "The Origins of Swedish Religious Organizations," 83.

15. There is ambiguity concerning the place of meetings after the first on the German vessel. Gracey states (*Missions*, 2:181) that Bergner began services in a rented one-room school four or five years after arriving in America. This is unlikely as it would have preceded his conversion and conflicts with all other available accounts. The probable date of Bergner's first service is sometime in 1844, a date also accepted by Lawson. Gracey also identifies the floating chapel used by Bergner as the one owned by the Protestant Episcopal Church, which he states was moored at Pier 11 on the North River. However, the Episcopal Floating Church of Our Saviour was located on the opposite side of Manhattan in the East River at the foot of Pike Street. The *John Wesley* was moored at Pier 11 on the North River. The place was correct, but he was mistaken about the ship.

16. *New York City Tract Society Annual Report for 1845*, 18 (now the New York City Mission Society).

17. *Sailor's Magazine*, December 1844, 122.

18. Ibid.

19. The Asbury Society, as a church extension organization, established the Asbury Church on Norfolk Street. Some sources have incorrectly attributed the purchase of the Bethel Ship to the Asbury Church, rather than the Asbury Society.

20. Seaman, *Annals*, 332.

21. *New York City Tract Society Annual Report for 1845*, 18.

22. The above mentioned basic sources relate the events leading to Hedstrom's decision and his appointment to the Bethel Ship.

23. Olof G. Hedstrom's first quarterly report to Rev. P. P. Sandford, Hedstrom's Presiding Elder, published in the *Christian Advocate and Journal*, 20, no. 8 (October 1, 1845): 30.

24. Hedstrom, "Bethel Ship—*John Wesley*," *Sailor's Magazine*, August 1846. Hedstrom's article, written as a report to the Seamen's Chaplains Convention, gives the origin and a brief survey of the Bethel Ship program.

25. The certificate of incorporation of the First North River Bethel Society of the Methodist Episcopal Church is preserved in the safe of the United Methodist Society, New York. Attached to the certificate is the hand-written and signed call to the meeting for the purpose of incorporation by Olof G. Hedstrom. The minutes of the meeting are also attached. The Immanuel United Methodist Church of 422 Dean Street, Brooklyn, New York, is the legal successor and still operates under the original certificate of incorporation, amended to change the name to the Immanuel Swedish Methodist Episcopal Church on January 18, 1883. Two groups in this church, a remnant of the Swedish congregation and a Spanish-speaking congregation, share the services of a bilingual pastor.

26. *New York City Tract Society Annual Report for 1849.*

27. Liljegren, Westergreen, and Wallenius, *Svenska Metodismen i Amerika*, 160. Bergner's final words were, "Now I go to see Him whom I have long desired to see."

28. *New York City Tract Society Annual Report for 1866*, 18.

6. *The Bethel Ship* John Wesley

1. Sven B. Newman, *Sjelfbiografi*, 61.

2. *Missionary Advocate*, 7, no. 9 (December 1851): 71.

3. *Christian Advocate and Journal*, 31, no. 111 (July 20, 1856): 28.

4. *Missionary Advocate*, 13 (July 1857): 30.

5. *The Sailor's Magazine* (April 1858), supplement: *Life Boat*, 30.

6. Wade Crawford Barclay, *The Methodist Episcopal Church: 1845–1939* (New York, 1957), 3:125, note.

7. Ibid.

8. Ibid., 272; Seaman, *Annals*, 332.

9. O. G. Hedstrom, report in *Christian Advocate and Journal*, 20, no. 8 (October 1, 1845): 30.

10. O. G. Hedstrom, *Missionary Advocate*, 2, no. 5 (August 1846): 36.

11. Minutes of the May 1845 meeting of the New York City Sunday School Society of the Methodist Episcopal Church. Minutes available at United Methodist City Society, 475 Riverside Drive, New York.

12. Seaman, *Annals*, 208; Robert W. Lynn and Eliott Wright, *The Big Little School* (Nashville: Abington Press, 1971), 35–38.

13. Lynn and Wright, *The Big Little School*, 54.

14. Hedstrom, *Christian Advocate and Journal*, 30.

15. Ibid.

16. Ibid. Hedstrom states, "The holy scriptures in Polish, German, Swedish, Norwegian, Danish, Italian, Portuguese, French and Spanish have been distributed from this ship by means of those excellent organizations, the Marine and New York Bible societies."

17. Paul F. Douglas, *The Story of German Methodism (Biography of an Immigrant Soul)* (New York and Cincinnati: The Methodist Book Concern, 1939), 9.

18. Hedstrom, *Christian Advocate and Journal*, 30.

19. Hedstrom, *Missionary Advocate*, 36.

20. Roald Kverndahl, *Seamen's Missions: Their Origin and Early Growth* (Pasadena, Cal.: William Carey Library, 1986), 515.

21. *Annual Report of the Missionary Society* (Methodist Church, 1949): 92.

22. Olsson, *Swedish Passenger Arrivals in New York*, 66–128; Paul Elmen, *Wheat Flour Messiah: Eric Jansson of Bishop Hill* (Carbondale, Ill.: Southern Illinois Univ. Press, 1976); Olov Isaksson and Soren Hallgren, *Bishop Hill: A Utopia on the Prairie* (Stockholm, Sweden:

L. T. Publishing House in Cooperation with Museum of National Antiquities and Swedish Pioneer Historical Society.
23. *Annual Report of the Missionary Society* (Methodist Church, 1848): 100.
24. Hedstrom, "Bethel Ship," 368.
25. *Missionary Advocate*, 36.

7. *From North River to Swedish Bethel*

1. Olsson, *Swedish Passenger Arrivals in New York*, 61. On the Cassel party, see the special issue, "Peter Cassel and New Sweden, Iowa," *Swedish Pioneer Historical Quarterly* (1981): 32; H. Arnold Barton, *The Search for Ancestors: A Swedish-American Family Saga* (Carbondale, Ill.: Southern Illinois Univ. Press, 1979), chap. 3.
2. Olsson, *Swedish Passenger Arrivals in New York*, 62, n. 91.
3. Ibid., 68, n. 91.
4. Wesley M. Westerberg, "Bethel Ship to Bishop Hill: Document, Letter of Olof Olsson," *Swedish Pioneer Historical Quarterly*, 23 (1972): 62.
5. Ibid.
6. Ibid., 63.
7. Elmen, *Wheat Flour Messiah*, 99.
8. *Annual Report of the Missionary Society* (Methodist Church, 1850).
9. Newman, *Sjelfbiografi*, 60.
10. Ibid., 23–28.
11. Ibid., 31.
12. Ibid., 68–69.
13. Ibid., 76.
14. Fredrick Kron, "Metodismens början bland Skandinaverna i New York och Brooklyn." *Sändebudet*, May 11, 1895. As Swedish Methodists prepared to celebrate the fiftieth anniversary of the Bethel Ship ministry and the founding of Swedish Methodism on May 25, 1845, Frederick Kron was requested to write his recollections. Having become a member of the Bethel Ship Sunday school at the age of nine in 1851, Kron had the longest record of association with the project. In addition, after arrival home from service

in the Civil War, Kron became a Bethel Ship class leader and a close confidant of Olof Hedstrom. The article has been placed in the Henry Whyman Swedish Methodist Collection, Drew University.

15. Ibid.

16. Rosenberg, *Religion and the Rise of the American City*, 2–3.

17. Peter Bergner, report in *Missionary Advocate*, 7 (December 1851): 71.

18. *Missionary Advocate*, 10, no. 7 (October 1854): 52–53.

19. Rosenberg, *Religion and the Rise of the American City*, 173.

20. [Magnus F.?] Hokansen, *Swedish Immigration in L's Time*, 51, n. 10, quote from "an immigrant letter." No source given.

21. Rosenberg, *Religion and the Rise of the American City*, 173.

22. *Missionary Advocate*, 10, no. 7 (October 1854).

23. *Annual Report of the Missionary Society* (Methodist Church, 1850), 77.

24. Kron, "Metodismens Början."

25. *Annual Report of the Missionary Society* (1850), 77.

26. *Missionary Advocate* (1851).

27. Kverndahl, *Seamen's Missions*, 198.

28. *Missionary Advocate* (March 1855).

29. *Christian Advocate and Journal*, 21:82. Letter dated April 1, 1853, to R. G. Stevens, secretary of the Tract Society of the Methodist Episcopal Church. *Annual Report of the Missionary Society* (1851): appropriation for printing in Swedish the general rules, ritual, and catechism of the Methodist church.

30. Jacob Bredberg, *Swedish Historical Society of America* (Minneapolis: Year Book, 1923–24), 94. Letter from Bredberg to Eric Norelius, February 9, 1854.

31. Bredberg to Norelius, 94.

32. *Annual Report of the Missionary Society* (1856).

33. *Annual Report of the Missionary Society* (1854 and 1855).

34. *Missionary Advocate* (May 1854).

35. Ibid. (February 1853).

36. *Christian Advocate and Journal*, 28, no. 1 (January 6, 1853).

37. Ibid., 35, no. 29 (July 19, 1860): 114.

38. Ibid. Sture Bolin, *En Skånsk Prästson i Amerika* (Lund: Gleerups Förlag, 1960), 47ff.

39. H. Arnold Barton, *Letters from the Promised Land: Swedes in America 1840–1914* (Minneapolis: Univ. of Minnesota Press, for the Swedish Pioneer Historical Society, 1975).

40. *Christian Advocate and Journal*, 20, no. 8 (October 1, 1845): 30.

41. Eric Norelius, *Svenska Luterska församlingar och Svenskarnas historia i Amerika*, 2 vols. (Rock Island, Ill.: Augustana Book Concern, 1890 and 1916), 1:33–34.

42. Ibid., 33.

43. Ibid.

44. Ibid., 34.

45. Kron, "Metodismens Början."

8. Jenny Lind

1. Allan Kastrup, *The Swedish Heritage in America* (St. Paul, Minn.: Swedish Council of America, 1975), 256–61.

2. Ibid., 256.

3. Ibid.

4. Ernest A. Spangberg, *Jenny Lind: The Swedish Nightingale and Her American Tour*, The Swedish Element in America, ed. Erik G. Westman, 4 vols. (Chicago, 1931–1934), 2:473–90. Cf. W. Porter Ware and Thaddeau C. Lockhard, Jr., *P. T. Barnum Presents Jenny Lind: The American Tour of the Swedish Nightingale* (Baton Rouge, La., 1980).

5. Newman, *Sjelfbiografi*, 86.

6. Witting, *Minnen*, 168–70.

7. Spangberg, *Jenny Lind*, 481–82.

8. Witting, *Minnen*, 169.

9. Kastrup, *Swedish Heritage*, 257.

10. Witting, *Minnen*, 168.

11. Ibid., 169.

12. The two Jenny Lind letters included in this chapter were originally in the possession of Rev. A. J. Anderson, pastor of the Brooklyn church that is the legal successor of the Bethel Ship. The church property was purchased in the name of the North River Bethel Society of the Methodist Episcopal Church. Anderson was pastor from 1880 to 1893, and it was during his tenure that

the charter was amended and the name changed to the Immanuel Swedish Methodist Church. The Lind letters were presented to the Immanuel church by Anderson's daughters and were subsequently placed in the Swedish Methodist Collection at Drew University.

13. *Annual Report of the Missionary Society* (1851), 61.

14. Newman, *Sjelfbiografi*, 86.

15. Kastrup, *Swedish Heritage*, 260.

16. Hedstrom, diary.

17. Spangberg, *Jenny Lind*, 2:488.

18. *Missionary Advocate*, 7 (December 1851): 71.

19. Witting, *Minnen*, 169.

9. Jonas Hedstrom Migrates West

1. Oliver A. Linder, *The Story of Illinois and the Swedish People. The Swedish Element in America*, ed. Erik G. Westman, 4 vols. (Chicago, 1931), 1:33.

2. Nottebäck parish records.

3. "The Love Feast," 77.

4. The New York Public Library. Many early Methodist church records are under custodial care, including records of the Second Street Methodist Church.

5. Olsson, *Swedish Passenger Arrivals in New York*, 12, 13 n. 57.

6. Witting, *Minnen*, 172.

7. Liljegren, Westergreen, and Wallenius, *Svenska Metodismen i Amerika*, 166.

8. Shirley Thompson Kelly, "Partially Completed Genealogical Survey of the Descendants of George Scornberger 1759–1841." In addition to forty-five manuscript pages of genealogical information, there is an alphabetical index of family names with twelve references to the Hedstrom family. A three-page, single-spaced foreword contains historic information about George Sornberger.

9. Allen De Long, town of Worcester historian, in a letter to Rev. William R. Phinney dated February 13, 1984, states: "I . . . find an Alexander Sornberger who was Overseer of Highways in the years 1833, 1835, and 1836."

10. *Dictionary of American History*, rev. ed., S.V. "Military tracts": warranties to Revolutionary War and War of 1812 veterans.

11. J. E. Temple, "Victoria Township." *Historical Encyclopedia of Illinois and Knox County* (1899): 828–29.

12. Kelly, "Genealogical Survey."

13. Witting, *Minnen*, 174.

14. Ibid.

15. Kelly, "Genealogical Survey." Witting, *Minnen*, 174. The sequence of marriage and moving to Victoria is somewhat confusing in Witting's account.

16. Kelly, "Genealogical Survey."

17. Temple, "Victoria Township," 828–29.

18. Witting, *Minnen*, 175.

19. Liljegren, Westergreen, and Wallenius, *Svenska Metodismen i Amerika*, 172.

20. Witting, *Minnen*, 178. Liljegren, Westergreen, and Wallenius, *Svenska Metodismen i Amerika*, 171.

21. Ibid., 169–71. Witting, *Minnen*, 178–79.

22. Liljegren, Westergreen, and Wallenius, *Svenska Metodismen i Amerika*, 171. Witting, *Minnen*, 180.

23. Witting, *Minnen*, 180. Liljegren, Westergreen, and Wallenius, *Svenska Metodismen i Amerika*, 171.

24. Witting, *Minnen*, 195–272; Liljegren, Westergreen, and Wallenius, *Svenska Metodismen i Amerika*, 257–69.

25. Witting, *Minnen*, 181–82.

26. Ibid., 183.

27. Ibid., 183–85.

28. Ibid., 183; Liljegren, Westergreen, and Wallenius, *Svenska Metodismen i Amerika*, 173–74.

10. Bishop Hill and Victor Witting

1. Elmen, *Wheat Flour Messiah*, 208–14. Elmen includes an exhaustive bibliography concerning Bishop Hill and its founder, Eric Jansson.

2. Ibid., 13.

3. Ibid., 60–76. Chapter 6, "The Burning of Books."

4. Wesley, *Christian Perfection*, 4, 56–57. Wesley, after reading

Thomas à Kempis (*Imitation of Christ*), William Law (*A Treatise on Christian Perfection*), and Jeremy Taylor (*The Rule and Exercise of Holy Living*), was, in his own words, "convinced more than ever of the impossibility of being half a Christian" (p. 4). He strove to live and promote holy living. Wesley defined sin as both voluntary and involuntary transgression. Concerning the latter he wrote, "I believe there is no such perfection in this life as excludes involuntary transgression, which I apprehend to be naturally consequent on the ignorance and mistakes inseparable from mortality. Therefore sinless perfection is a phrase I never use" (p. 57). Eric Jansson preached that persons, once saved and forgiven, entered an enduring state of Christian perfection, including actions in the future, without regard to standards and consequences. Theologically, this is called the heresy of antinomianism and historically has surfaced from time to time. Lutherans were justifiably sensitive to the possibility of an antinomian interpretation of the "holiness" preached by the Hedstroms and Methodists. Erik Norelius complained that Olof Hedstrom confused the law and the gospel. Lars P. Esbjörn accused Jonas Hedstrom of pandering to the Janssonists. The semantics were similar—the interpretation very different.

5. Elmen, *Wheat Flour Messiah*, 79–80.

6. Hurtig, *Metodistkyrkan i Sverige 100 År*, 98. Liljegren, Westergreen, and Wallenius, *Svenska Metodismen i Amerika*, 323–47.

7. Erik Johnson and C. F. Peterson, *Svenskarna i Illinois* (Chicago: W. Williamson, 1880). Johnson was Eric Jansson's son. Elmen, *Wheat Flour Messiah*, 100.

8. Elmen, *Wheat Flour Messiah*, 124.

9. Ibid., 124. Erik Johnson, "The Swedish Colony at Bishop Hill," *Viking*, vol. 1 (March 1907): 9–10, 18–19.

10. *New York City Directory*, 1845, 1846, 1847, New York Public Library.

11. Elmen, *Wheat Flour Messiah*, 146.

12. Erik G. Westman, ed. *The Swedish Element in America*. 4 vols. 1:42. Linder, *The Story of Illinois*, 33.

13. Linder, *The Story of Illinois*, 33–42.

14. Witting, *Minnen*, 40–48.

15. Ibid., 55–62.

16. Ibid., 62.

17. Elmen, *Wheat Flour Messiah*, 104. Cf. Erik Wiken, "New Light on the Erik Janssonists' Emigration," *Swedish American Historical Quarterly*, 35 (1984): 221–38, and errata, ibid., 36 (1985): 68–69.

18. Witting, *Minnen*, 259–60.

19. Liljegren, Westergreen, and Wallenius, *Svenska Metodismen i Amerika*, 200; Johnson and Peterson, *Svenskarne i Illinois*, 35.

20. Elmen, *Wheat Flour Messiah*, 140–44; Gustaf Unonius was a well-educated idealist who emigrated with a small group of like-minded persons and settled in Wisconsin. His enthusiastic correspondence, published in Sweden's *Aftonbladet*, encouraged further migration. Unonius was later ordained a priest in the Episcopal church and founded the Swedish Episcopal church in Chicago.

21. Witting, *Minnen*, 65f.

22. Henry Emanuel Whyman, "In Memoriam—Catharina Witting," September 12, 1901, an eight-page biographical eulogy delivered at her memorial service, Quinsigamond Swedish Methodist Church, Worcester, Mass. It is printed in pamphlet form, in all probability published by her husband, Rev. Victor Witting. The format and type are similar to his *Minnen*. The monograph is deposited in the Swedish Methodist Collection at Drew University. Olsson, *Swedish Passenger Arrivals in New York*, 146–47. Olof Olsson had apparently assumed his father's name, Lind, when he arrived in America, as recorded in the ship's manifest. While Nils Olsson does not identify the young woman listed on the manifest as Karin Dahlsten (Dahlström) as the future Catharina Witting, there can be no doubt that she is the same person. Witting, *Minnen*, 107–9.

23. Whyman, "In Memoriam."

24. Witting, *Minnen*, 126–34. See this work for Witting's account of his financially disastrous business venture in New York and his accompanying spiritual crisis in which an inner voice seemed to be saying, "Do you remember the night of the *Ceres* shipwreck? Do you remember the Holy Communion? Do you remember the promises made to the Lord—that if your life was spared you would become a Christian? Have you kept your promise? Broken promises— BROKEN PROMISES." Witting relates the story of his conversion, subsequent counseling by Hedstrom on the Bethel Ship, and the beginning of his ministry.

11. From Ship to Scandinavian Shores

1. *Annual Report of the Missionary Society* (1852), 623.
2. Ibid. (1849), 92.
3. Ibid. (1851), 23.
4. Thunström, *Olof Gustaf Hedstrom*, 39–44.
5. Witting, *Minnen*.
6. Thunström, *Hedstrom*, 43–44.
7. *Annual Report of the Missionary Society* (1855), 57. Barclay, *Methodist Episcopal Church, 1845–1939* (New York: The Board of Missions of the Methodist Church, 1957), 3:957.
8. *Annual Report of the Missionary Society* (1851), 45–46; Sven M. Swenson had made a fortune from Texas real estate. He later established himself as a New York banker and cotton broker while also operating the S M S Ranch in Texas. Olsson, *Swedish Passenger Arrivals*, 18n.
9. Andersen, *The Salt of the Earth*, 27–29.
10. Odd Hagen, *Preludes to Methodism in Northern Europe* (Oslo, Norway: Norsk Förlagsselskap, 1981), 50–51.
11. Barclay, *The Methodist Episcopal Church*, 3:935–46.
12. Ibid., 3:934.
13. Andersen, *Salt of the Earth*, 18–19.
14. Barclay, *The Methodist Episcopal Church*, 3:946–47.
15. Ibid., 601.
16. Witting, *Minnen*, 515.
17. Ibid., 527.
18. Ibid., 526.
19. Ibid., 520.
20. Ibid., 522.
21. Ibid., 528.
22. *Christian Advocate and Journal*, July 23, 1863.
23. *Annual Report of the Missionary Society* (1867). In addition to Karlskrona and Nättraby, the work in Gothenburg is directly attributable to Hedstrom's preaching and labors.
24. Ibid.
25. Witting, *Minnen*, 536–37. Witting includes the text of Durbin's letter of appointment as district superintendent on behalf of Bishop Kingsley, as well as his reply.

26. Ibid., 536. He begins the organization and structure of local Methodist churches.

27. Ibid., 540.

28. Ibid.

29. Barclay, *The Methodist Episcopal Church*, 968. Erikson, *Svenska Metodismen i Sverige*, 276. The Dissenter Law took effect October 31, 1873.

30. Witting, *Minnen*, 566–72.

31. Ibid., 569–71.

32. Ibid., 566. Erikson, *Svenska Metodismen i Sverige*, 276. Both sources provide a complete text of the royal resolution signed by Oscar II and contain the substance of the preliminary interview.

12. An Accomplished Mission

1. In recounting the Bethel Ship saga, I have often thought of Frank Dahnson, my only direct contact with the Bethel Ship. Nothing delighted him more than an opportunity to talk about the Bethel Ship and Olof Hedstrom. As his pastor, I called upon him in the hospital after an accident. On a second visit a day or two later, Frank had been moved to a private room. His greeting was typical: "When I saw you last I was in steerage. Now I am in first class—and soon I shall be in the pilot house with the Captain." His experiences of life and faith were generally expressed in nautical terms.

Index

Henry C. Whyman, a retired Methodist minister, received a M.Div. from Union Theological Seminary in New York and a Ph.D. from New York University. After thirty-two years of parish work, he was appointed to administrative positions in the New York Conference of the United Methodist Church. During the last thirteen years he has served as the executive of the United Methodist City Society with responsibilities for urban ministries. He is the author of *The History of Ethnic Ministries in the New York Conference, The United Methodist Church.*